STUDENT BOOK

WORKPLACE ENGLISH
Office File

Marc Helgesen

Keith Adams

LONGMAN

Longman Group Limited,
Longman House, Burnt Mill, Harlow,
Essex CM20 2JE, England
and Associated Companies throughout the world.

© Longman Group Limited 1995

First published 1995

ISBN 0 582 27666 7

Set in Helvetica 11/13

Printed in Singapore

Acknowledgements

We are grateful to the following for permission to
reproduce these copyright photographs:

© Longman Group/Gareth Boden for pages 38 &
57; Pictor International for page 78 (top left); Tony
Stone Images/Dan Bosler for page 78 (top right).

All photographs not listed above are © Longman
Group/Tony Hertz.

Cover photograph © Longman Group/Trevor
Clifford

Illustrated by:
Julie Anderson, Kathy Baxendale, Phil Dobson,
Neil Gower, Paul Hampson, Conny Jude,
Tim Kahane, Frances Lloyd, Colin Mier, 1-11 Line
Art, Steve Noon, Tech Type, Andrew Thorpe,
Kevin White, Allen Whittert.

We wish to thank the following people for their
assistance, suggestions, encouragement and
testing of the material.
Rube Redfield, Otemai Junior College, Hyogo;
Ellen Shaw, University of Nevada;
Steve Brown, University of Pittsburgh;
Masako Kirihara and Sean O'Brien, ECC, Osaka;
Tadakuni Tajiri, Masanori Nishi, Takuya Okamoto,
YMCA, Osaka;
Sharon Setoguchi, Riverside Public Schools,
California;
Elizabeth Nichols, James English School, Sendai;
Gerald Couzens, Brenda Hayashi, Hiroyuki
Miyawaki, Michiko Wako, Yoko Hakuta, Yoko
Futami, Miyagi Gakuin, Sendai;
Kevin Bergman, Tokyo;
Shinsuke Suzuki, Apple Books, Tokyo;
Noriko Fukaya, Maria "Indy" Nepomuceno, Jinno
Pacific College, Nagoya

Thanks to the many people at Longman for their
assistance and encouragement. They include
Catherine Prentice, Gill Negus, Jeremy Osborne,
Paul Rust, Takashi Hala, Jung Ja Lee, Steve
Martin, Steve Galloway, Chris Balderston,
Cheryl McCarron, Kiyomi Kuji, Meiko Otaka,
Hiromi Tsuchiya, Kazuyo Saito, Reiko Murota,
Machiko Kan.

Special thanks to Janet Aitchison for guidance
and editorial insights and to Robyn Alton (Editor),
Jenny Fleet (Designer) and Yolanda Durham for
making the book happen.

Finally, we would also like to thank our students,
who made the project worthwhile, and our fami-
lies, Masumi and Kent Helgesen and Pensri
Adams for their support.

Introduction to students

MEMO

To: Students using *Workplace English: Office File*

From: Marc Helgesen and Keith Adams

Re: Using this book

We hope you enjoy using *Workplace English: Office File*.

This book will help you learn the English that you need to work in banks, hotels, travel agencies and airlines. Actually, because of international travel and business, English will help you in nearly any job.

The key to learning English is to communicate. *Workplace English: Office File* will help you build English skills. You will communicate with other students. You'll use English in many different business situations.

There are 18 units and 2 review sections in this book. Each unit contains:

- *Get ready!* Learning English is a little like learning a sport or learning music - you have to "do the activity." Like music or sports, it helps to "warm up" first. The warm-up activity will help you to get ready for each unit.

- *Conversation* The conversations are examples of English in business situations. There are "changes" in each conversation. Practice the conversation. Then try to use your own ideas for "changes."

- *Listening* The recordings are at natural speed. That's important. Most of the English speakers you meet at work don't speak slowly or clearly. Remember, you don't need to understand every word. When you listen, think about what you need to know. Listen for that information.

- *Pair Work or Group Work* Speaking to each other in pairs or groups is more than just practice. You will share information and really communicate. Remember the key is to speak in English.

- *Writing Right* You will practice writing letters, faxes and memos in English. The samples can also be used as a model when you need to write something for work.

- *Numbers* You probably already know the numbers in English. However, most students need more practice. The numbers sections will help you "use" numbers quickly.

We're sure you will make progress using English in your job. English, like any language, is for communication. That's what makes it interesting and fun.

Good luck. Enjoy using English!

Contents

1 Introductions

1 Here are some things people say when they introduce themselves.

Hello. I'm Mari Davis.

What do you do, Jim?

I work for Union Bank.

It's nice to meet you.

Hi. I'm Jim Wright.

I'm a student. And you?

I'm glad to meet you, too.

2 Introduce yourself to at least three people.

Conversation

Hello. My name's ...

1 Listen.

Good morning. Can I help you?

Yes, my name's _____. (name)

Good afternoon.
Hello.

Oh, yes. You're the new clerk. How do you do? I'm _____. (name)

It's nice to meet you.

It's nice to meet you.
Pleased to meet you.

I'm glad
It's good

Let me call Ms. Lee. She's our manager.

Thank you.

director
boss

All right.
Fine.

Pronunciation focus

2 Listen again. Say the sentences. Match the stress and rhythm.

3 Practice the conversation with a partner.
Then close your book. Have a conversation like this one.

It's Culture

Meeting people
In English-speaking countries, remember:
- Look at the person's eyes. If you don't, it gives a bad impression (feeling).
- Shake hands firmly (but not *too* strongly).
- Handshakes only last 2 or 3 seconds.

How do you greet people in your country?

Listening 📼

What's your phone number?

1 📼 Listen. Check (✔) the names, addresses, and phone numbers you hear.

1. ☐ Oscar Brown
   ☑ Oscar Braun

2. ☐ Sue Nielsen
   ☐ Sue Nelson

3. ☐ 815 East Ave.
   ☐ 850 East Ave.

4. ☐ (022) 374-4588
   ☐ (022) 347-4508

5. ☐ 1200 First St., Room 70
   ☐ 1220 First St. Room 17

2 📼 Listen. Fill in the forms.

1.

WORLD AIRWAYS

RECONFIRMATION

Flight Number: WA 821

Date: May 15

Passenger's Name: MR. MS.   Knight,
_____
                     last   first

Phone: _____

2.

NEW ACCOUNT APPLICATION   **First Bank**

Name: MR. MS. R _____ G _____
              last   first

Home Address: 591 _____

              Vancouver, B.C. _____

Nationality: _____

3.

HORIZON TRAVEL

NAME: _____
        (family)   (first)

NATIONALITY: _____

PASSPORT NUMBER: _____

OCCUPATION: _____

Pair Work A 👥

Where are you from?

Student A, use this page. Student B, use activity file 39 on page 92 in the back of the book.

What's	Ms. Reed's Mr. Lee's your	first name?	It's		Maya. Sam. ...
Where	is	she he	from?	She's He's	from	Seattle. Taipei. ......
	are	you		I'm		......
Where	does	she he	work? go to school?	At		Intertech Software. Union Bank. ......
	do	you				
What	does	she he	do?	She's He's	a	secretary. bank teller.
	do	you		I'm		student.

1 **Fill in the cards. Ask B for the information you need.**

Hometown:

Company:

Position:

Maya Reed

Hometown:

Company:

Position:

da Silva

Hometown:
Taipei
Company:
Union Bank

Position:
Bank Teller

Sam Lee

Your partner (B).

Hometown:

Company/school:

Name:

Position:

Part-time job:

Hometown:
Toronto
Company:
Toronto Business
College
Position:
Student
Part-time job:
Campus Books

Naomi Sato

- - - Keep going! - - - - ➤

2 **Your pair joins another pair. Introduce your partner.**

This is _____. She's a _____.

Listen to the introductions of the other pair. Ask more questions. Try to learn at least two things about each person.

Writing Right ✏️

Business letters

1 Read this business letter. Answer the questions.

1. What is the writer's name?
_____

2. Where does the writer work?
_____

3. Who is the letter to?
_____

2 Look at the letter again. Label these parts.
- ◼ *date*
- ◼ *body* = the message
- ◼ *closing*
- ◼ *greeting*
- ◼ *inside address* = the reader's name and address
- ◼ *letterhead* = includes the writer's company name, address, phone and fax numbers
- ◼ *signature* = should be *signed*, not printed
- ◼ *writer's name*
- ◼ *writer's job*
- ◼ *enc.* = enclosures (something is being sent with the letter)

Intertech
S O F T W A R E

249 Ocean Street
Seattle
Washington 98239
U.S.A.

Phone: (206) 555-2378
Fax: (206) 555-3894

April 25, (year)

Ms. Maki Ito
Manager
World Travel
1-7-32 Honcho
Chuo-ku, Osaka 541 Japan

Dear Ms. Ito:

Thank you for using Intertech Software's services in the past.

Enclosed is a copy of our new catalog. Our new program, **Astrowrite**, is one of the best word processing systems available.

Please let me know if you would like more information or a demonstration.

I look forward to hearing from you.

Sincerely,

Roy Green

Roy Green
Sales Representative

enc.

Numbers 1.2.3.

Numbers are important in almost every type of business. When do you use numbers?

1 📼 Listen. On a piece of paper, write the numbers you hear. Then check by saying the numbers. Your teacher will write them on the board.

2 📼 Listen. You will hear the numbers in sentences. Write only the numbers. Check by saying the numbers. Your teacher will write them.

3 👥 Student A, use activity file 1 (page 82). Student B, use activity file 20 (page 87).

2 Clarifying meaning

- - - - - - - - - - - - - *Get ready!* **- - - - - - - - - - - -**

1 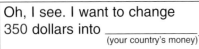 **Work with a partner. What do you say when:**
- you want someone to say something again?
- you don't understand something?

Write as many sentences as you can.

EXAMPLES: Excuse me?
Could you...

Say the sentences. Your teacher will write them on the board.

2 **Pretend you are saying the sentences. Move your mouth but don't make any sound. Partner, how fast can you guess the sentences? Take turns.**

Conversation

What does that mean?

1 **Listen.**

A. Excuse me. I'd like to change some money. — Fine. Into what currency?

exchange

B. Pardon? What does that mean? — Currency? What kind money do you want?

do you
does "currency"

would you like
do you need

Oh, I see. I want to change 350 dollars into _____.
(your country's money)

I'm sorry? Did you say 315 or 350?

315

Pardon?
Excuse me?

350. Three-five-oh.

350? I see. Could you fill out this form, please?

315. Three-one-five

OK.
All right.

Pronunciation focus

2 **Listen again. Say the sentences. Match the stress and rhythm.**

3 **Practice the conversation with a partner.**
Then close your book. Have a conversation like this one.

Listening 📻

When you don't understand, ask!

1 📻 **Listen. What does the second speaker say? Write the phrases.**

1. You need to get a *furikae* form over there.

   How do you say (that) in English?

2. Write your name on the top line.

   _____ _____ ?

3. Could I ask you to sign your name at the bottom?

   _____ ?

4. The name's Wilkenson.

   _____ _____ _____ _____ ?

5. My name's Terry Wilkenson.

   _____ _____ _____ _____ (_____)?

6. It only costs 40 dollars.

   _____ _____ _____ (_____) _____ (_____)?

7. Turn right, then the next left, then right again. Got it?

   _____ _____ _____ .

8. Can you tell me how late it is going to be?

   _____ _____ _____ .

2 📻 **Listen. Which phrases do they say?**
Check (✔) the phrases above as you hear them.

Pair Work A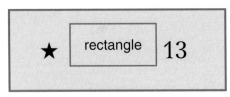

Understanding what you hear

Student B, use activity file 40 (page 93).

1. How do you spell it?
2. What does that mean?
3. Could you repeat that?
4. How do you say that in English?
5. I don't understand.

6. I don't know.
7. Pardon?
8. Excuse me?
9. Did you say 14 or 40?

1 **Work with B. Which phrases do you use for each problem?**
Write the numbers.
What do you say when:
a. you want someone to say something again?   _3_ , ___ or ___
b. you don't know how to write a word?   ___
c. you don't know the meaning of a word?   ___
d. you don't know how to say a word in English?   ___
e. you aren't sure which number you heard?   ___
f. you don't know the meaning of a question?   ___
g. you don't know the answer to a question?   ___

2 **Close your book. B will ask questions. Say the correct phrases.**
Then B will close the book. Ask the questions from exercise 1.
Use this order: d - f - a - c - g - e - b. B will answer.

What do you say when you don't know how to say a word in English?

3 **Read the instructions below. Answer B's questions. B will draw this picture.**

★	rectangle	13

1. Draw a rectangle.
2. Write the word "rectangle" in it.
3. (speak very softly) Draw a star to the left of the rectangle.
4. (speak very fast) Write "thirteen" to the right of the rectangle.

Now, follow B's instructions. Draw the picture in the box.
When you don't understand, ask.
Use the phrases in the blue box.

- - - *Keep going!* - - - ➡

4 **Think of the job you have or will have someday.**
■ Where do you work?
■ What do you like about the job?
■ What don't you like about the job?
■ What things are difficult?
Tell B about the job. Answer B's questions.

5 **Then listen to B. Use the phrases in the blue box.**
When you use one, check it (✔).

Writing Right 🖎
Fix the letter

Maki Ito is the manager of World Travel in Osaka, Japan. She wrote this letter to Roy Green. He is a sales representative for Intertech Software.

1 **Put the letter in the right order by numbering the parts (1–14). There are two extra pieces. You don't need them. Write X in those boxes.**

I am writing to ask if it is possible to receive a sample of the **Astrowrite** program. Also, please send a price list for all the programs.

Love,

1-7-32 Honcho
Chuo-ku
Osaka 541
Japan

Phone: 06-238-9387
Fax: 06-298-0384

Sales representative

Maki Ito

WORLD TRAVEL

Intertech Software
249 Ocean Street
Seattle
Washington 98239
U.S.A.

Dear Mr. Green:

Sincerely,

May 9, (year)

I look forward to hearing from you.

Maki Ito

Thank you for the Intertech Software catalog which you sent recently. The programs look interesting and useful.

Maki Ito

Mr. Roy Green

Manager

2 **You try! Make a company letterhead. Write a letter to Roy Green. Thank him for the catalog. Ask if it is possible to have a demonstration of Astrowrite. When you finish, check the business letter on page 9. Did you remember all the parts?**

3 **Look at activity file 72 (page 110). Then fold your letter. Address an envelope to Mr. Green.**

Numbers 1.2.3.

1 🔊 **Listen. On a piece of paper, write the numbers you hear. Then check by saying the numbers. Your teacher will write them on the board.**

2 🔊 **Listen. You will hear the numbers in sentences. Write only the numbers. Check by saying the numbers. Your teacher will write them.**

3 👥 **Student A, use activity file 2 (page 82). Student B, use activity file 21 (page 87).**

3 Comparing jobs

- - - - - - - - - *Get ready!* - - - - - - - - -

1 👥👥👥 **Work in groups of four. What jobs do you know in English?
How many jobs can your team write for each group?**

Jobs				
that have high pay	that are exciting	where you need a lot of training	that are dangerous	that have high status
lawyer				

Conversation 💬

I'm going to become a...

1 📻 **Listen.**

I'm going to become a computer programmer.

A programmer? I thought you wanted to work at a bank.

Well, a programmer's job is more interesting than a bank teller's.

Yes, but it is more difficult.

A

study to be	were going to
be	planned to

B

challenging	takes more training
exciting	is more work

But think of the higher pay.

I guess so.

What are you going to do?

I don't know yet. Being a store clerk is OK for now.

C

higher status	I can see that.
better future	That's true.

D

be	salesperson
study for	student

Pronunciation focus

2 📻 **Listen again. Say the sentences. Match the stress and rhythm.**

3 👥 **Practice the conversation with a partner.
Then close your book. Have a conversation like this one.**

Listening 📻
What do you think?

Remember!

■ Short adjectives take **er**:
high pay → high**er** pay

■ Long adjectives (two or more syllables) take **more**:
dangerous → **more** dangerous

■ Adjectives that end in **y** change to **ier**:
easy → eas**ier**

1 📻 **Listen. Finish the sentences. When you hear the tone, write the name of a job. Write jobs you don't think other students will write.**

EXAMPLE: A _doctor_ gets high_er_ pay than a _____ .

1. It's _____ difficult to be a _____ than a _____ .

2. Being a _____ safe _____ .

3. _____ better at typing _____ .

4. _____ has high___ status _____ .

5. _____ easy _____ .

6. _____ dangerous _____ .

2 **Work in groups of three. Compare answers.**

A: What did you write?
B: I wrote, "A doctor gets higher pay than a nurse."
A: I wrote the same thing.
C: I wrote, "A doctor gets higher pay than a teacher."

It's Culture

Job titles
Some job names are changing. The new names show men and women both do the job.

EXAMPLES:

Old name	New name
stewardess/steward	flight attendant
policeman/woman	police officer
actor/actress	actor
waitress/waiter	server

Do job titles in your country indicate men or women?

Group Work

Which occupation?

1 Work in groups of three. One student thinks of a job. The other students try to guess. When the guess is wrong, give a hint:

A: Is it the bank teller?   B: No, the person gets high**er** pay than a bank teller.
A: Is it the business person?   B: No, it's **more** exciting than being a business person.
C: Is it the athlete?   B: No, it's **less** dangerous than being an athlete.
A: Is it the TV announcer?   B: That's right!

store clerk

tour guide

doctor

bank teller

musician

teacher

mechanic

TV announcer

police officer

flight attendant

athlete

truck driver

business person   computer programmer   server
(waiter/waitress)

Ideas

is ...
difficult
easy
challenging
dangerous
safe
interesting
boring
clean
dirty

gets ...
higher/lower pay

has ...
higher/lower status

needs ...
training
to be intelligent
to be good (better) at:
    typing
    using a computer

— — Keep going! — — — — — →

2 Think of other jobs not on this page. Keep playing.

Writing Right 🖊
Find the mistakes

1 Read the letter. The writer made a lot of mistakes. Circle the mistakes.

MODERN PRODUCTIONS

23490 59th Street
San Francisco
CA 94608

Phone: 415-223-0000
Fax:415-223-1111

The New Asia Hotel
67 Ho Ping East Rd.
Section 1, Taipei
Taiwan
Ms. Ruth Chung
Reservation Manager

Dear Ms. Chung:

It is summer and has been warm and rainy. I hope you are having good weather.

I will be visiting Taiwan on business in October.

I look forward to hearing from you.

Send me information about room prices.

Love,

Tony Kaku

Tony Kaku
Clerk
June 9

2 You try! You are a clerk of a company. You will be in Taipei from October 21–24. You want to find out the cost of a single room. Write a letter to The New Asia Hotel.

Numbers 👥

1 📻 Listen. On a piece of paper, write the numbers you hear. Then check by saying the numbers.

2 📻 Listen. You will hear the numbers in sentences. Write only the numbers. Check by saying them.

3 👥 Student A, use activity file 3 (page 82). Student B, use activity file 22 (page 87).

4 Asking about ability

— Get ready! —

1 👥 **Work with a partner. Choose one of these jobs:**

bank teller flight attendant hotel clerk salesperson
secretary teacher tour guide travel agent

2 Anwer these questions. Write as many answers as possible in five minutes.

- What skills are needed for the job?

  A _____ can ...

- What does a person in that job like to do?

  She likes to ...

- What is that person good at doing?

  He is good at ...

Ideas
can type
can use a computer
can speak a foreign language
likes to meet people
likes to travel
is good at math
is good at public speaking

Conversation 💬

I can do that.

1 📻 **Listen.**

part-time job
new job

use a computer   office clerk
do math (mathematics)   bank teller

a little Chinese   travel
some Spanish   sell things

Not really.   hotel clerk
It's OK.   sales rep
                          (sales representative)

Pronunciation focus

2 📻 **Listen again. Say the sentences. Match the stress and rhythm.**

3 👥 **Practice the conversation with a partner.**
Then close your book. Have a conversation like this one.

Listening 🔊

Can you use a computer?

1 🔊 Listen. Write the information on the lines. What jobs do they want?
Check (✔) your answers.

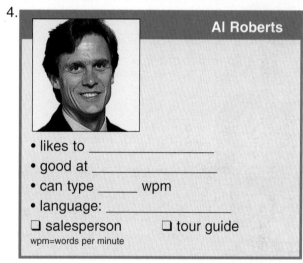

1.

James Williams

- can *use a computer*
- likes to _____
- language: _____
- ❏ travel agent   ❏ tour guide

3.

S.J. Kim

- can _____
- can type _____ wpm
- likes to _____
- language: _____
- ❏ hotel clerk   ❏ secretary

wpm=words per minute

2.

Ruth Lee

- good at _____
- can type _____ wpm
- language: _____
- ❏ secretary   ❏ bank teller

wpm=words per minute

4.

Al Roberts

- likes to _____
- good at _____
- can type _____ wpm
- language: _____
- ❏ salesperson   ❏ tour guide

wpm=words per minute

2 🔊 Listen to the questions. Write the answers about *yourself*. Use these symbols:

✔ = Yes   ✗ = No   ● = a little   ? = I don't know

1. _____
2. _____
3. _____
4. _____
5. _____
6. _____

7. _____

Pair Work A

The best job for you

Student B use activity file 41 (page 94).

1 Fill in the chart. Ask B for the information.

> ✔ = Yes   ✗ = No   ● = a little   ? = He/she doesn't know
> I don't know.

	Can she …? Can he…? Can you…?			Does she like…? Does he like …? Do you like…?		Is she good at…? Is he good at …? Are you good at…?		
	type	use a computer	speak another language	to meet people	to travel	math	selling things	public speaking
Karen	✔ 75 wpm*	✔	● *She can speak a little Portuguese*	✗			?	✗
Carl	✔ 65 wpm	✔			✗	✔	✗	
Sofia	✗ 10 wpm			✔	✔	●		
Ken	___ wpm	✔	● Japanese	✔		✔	?	✗
Jan	___ wpm	✔	✗		✔			●
B, your partner	___ wpm							

*wpm = words per minute. Karen can type 75 words in one minute.

2 With B, decide on one job for each person. Write the job next to the name.

tour guide   hotel clerk   bank clerk
travel agent   secretary   salesperson   Other:_____

┌ ─ ─*Keep going!*─ ─ ─ ─ ➤

**3 Find at least three job skills (typing, using a computer, etc.) you
and B both have. Then find at least three skills B has that you don't.**

Writing Right 🖎
A résumé

A résumé tells about your education. It also tells about your work experience and skill.

1 Read about Jerry Sanchez. Complete Jerry's résumé.

❝My name is Jerry Sanchez. I live at 1405 Bay Street, Honolulu, Hawaii, 96811. My phone number is 808-555-3416. I was born on June 12, 1975. I graduated from Pacific High School in 1993. Three years ago, I started at Honolulu City College. I am studying Business Administration. I will graduate next June. I have a part-time job at Tower Records. I'm a clerk. I'm good at typing (65 wpm) and I can use a computer. I speak two foreign languages: Spanish (advanced) and Japanese (elementary).❞

```
Jerry Sanchez
1405 _____
_____
_____

Phone: _____

Date of Birth: _____

Employment objective:
To work for a trading company.

Education:
College:
Honolulu City College.
Major: Business Administration,
September, _____ to present.
Will graduate _____.
High School:
_____,
Graduated, June 19__.

Work Experience:
1993 to present. _____ , _____ ,
                  (job)     (company)
Honolulu (part time).

Other information:
    Business skills:
    Good _____( ___ wpm)
    _____ skills
Languages:Spanish ( _____ )

(Elementary)          _____

References on request.
```

2 Now, write your résumé.

3 A "letter of application" is the letter you send with a résumé.
Look at activity file 71 (page 109).
Write a letter of application.

Numbers 1.2.3.

1 🔊 Listen. Check (✔) the numbers you hear.
❏ 12 ❏ 13 ❏ 14 ❏ 15 ❏ 16 ❏ 17 ❏ 18 ❏ 19
❏ 20 ❏ 30 ❏ 40 ❏ 50 ❏ 60 ❏ 70 ❏ 80 ❏ 90
Check by saying the numbers.

2 🔊 Listen. You will hear the numbers in sentences. Write only the numbers. Check by saying them.

3 👥 Student A, use activity file 4 (page 82). Student B, use activity file 23 (page 87).

5 Hotel check-in

- - - - - Get ready! - - - - -

1 Work in groups of three.
Student A, look at activity file 47 on page 100.
Student B, look at activity file 54 on page 102.
Student C, look at activity file 61 on page 104.
One person reads the first hint. The other two race to say the word.
EXAMPLE: A: A room with 2 beds.   B or C: It's a twin.
If you don't know the word in English, ask:
How do you say _____ in English?

Conversation

Could I ask your name?

1 Listen.

ma'am   three nights   twin   price for a twin
                                     two nights   suite   charge for a suite

$125.00   Would you mind filling   health club
$250.00   Would you fill   swimming pool

Pronunciation focus

2 Listen again. Say the sentences. Match the stress and rhythm.

3 Practice the conversation with a partner.
Then close your book. Have a conversation like this one.

22

Listening 🔊

Making a reservation

Paula Jackson is making a hotel reservation.

1 👥 🔊 **Work with a partner. Look at the hotel reservation form.**
What do you think the hotel clerk will ask? Write the questions.
Then listen. Were you right?

1. What's *your name* please?
2. Could _____ _____ _____ _____ _____ ?
3. And _____ _____ _____ ?
4. May I ask _____ _____ ?
5. How _____ _____ _____ _____ staying?
6. Would you like a _____ , a _____ ,or a _____ ?
7. Would _____ prefer _____ or _____ ?
8. How will _____ _____ paying?

2 🔊 **Listen. Fill in the information about Ms. Jackson.**

Flamingo Arms Hotel

Guest reservation

1. Name: Jackson,   Paula
   _____
              Last   First

2. Address: 420 West Bay Street
   _____
             San Francisco, CA
   _____

3. Telephone: _____

4. Nationality: _____

5. Arrive: 12 / 15   Depart: /

6. Room type:
   ❏ Single $ 85.00
   ❏ Twin $100.00
   ❏ Double $125.00

7. ❏ Smoking   ❏ Non-smoking

8. Method of payment:
   ❏ Cash
   ❏ Credit card: Viz   Gold Success
   Card Number: _____ Expiration date: _____

Pair Work A 👥

I'd like a room.

Student B, use activity file 42 (page 95).

1 You are a clerk at the Plaza Hotel. B is a guest.
Fill in the form for B. Answer B's questions.

The Plaza Hotel

How do you
spell _____ ?
(that)

Guest registration

Name: _____
     Last   First
Address: _____
_____
Telephone: _____
Nationality: _____
Arrive: /   Depart: /
Room type:
   ❑ Single
   ❑ Double $95.00
   ❑ Suite $110.00
                     $200.00
   ❑ Smoking   ❑ Non-smoking
Method of payment:
   ❑ Cash
   ❑ Credit card   Viz   Gold   Success
                  Card Number _____
Customer's signature: _____

Could you
repeat that?

Check out time: 11:00 a.m.
Hotel services: . . . . .Phone number:
   Front desk 04
   Room service (7:00 a.m. - 2:00 a.m.) 07
   Wake up calls 05
Restaurant: 24th floor
Business Center: 23rd floor
Pool: 20th floor

2 Now, you are the guest. You are checking into the Lakeview Hotel.
Ask about the prices. Decide the room you want.
Answer B's questions. Ask these questions:
◼ Where's the restaurant?
◼ Is there a sauna?
◼ What time is check out?
◼ How do I get room service?

Keep going!

**3 Close your book. With B, how many things from the form can
you remember? What other items are on hotel registration
forms in your country? How would you ask for this information?
Write one question for each item.**

Writing Right 📝
Faxing for information

1 Read the fax quickly. Then read it again. Find words for each meaning:

1. about: _____

2. prices: _____

3. money the agent receives: _____

4. the cost for more than one person: _____

5. things at the hotel such as a swimming pool, restaurants, etc: _____

Sunshine Travel Agency

34-2 Leewha-Dong   Tel: (82) 2-335-7987
Dongrae-ku   Fax: (82) 2-335-7988
Seoul 121-210 Korea

Fax message
If you do not receive all pages, call or fax immediately

To: Koala Hotel   **Date:** June 15, (year)
          Reservations Department
          Melbourne

From: S.J.Park
          Sunshine Travel

Re: Hotel information

Dear sir or madam:
We would appreciate receiving information about
your hotel's facilities including restaurant(s)
and meeting rooms as well as room charges. We
also need to know about group rates and the
travel agent's commission.
We look forward to hearing from you.
Sincerely,

S.J.Park

S.J.Park

2 Write a similar fax to The Union Bank. You want information about foreign currency accounts. Also ask about types of accounts, interest rates, bank charges and how to open an account.

Numbers 1.2.3.

1 🔊 Listen. Write the numbers you hear. Check by saying the numbers.

2 🔊 Listen. You will hear the numbers in sentences. Write only the numbers. Check by saying them.

3 👥 Student A, use activity file 5 (page 83). Student B, use activity file 24 (page 88).

6 Office routines

- - - - - - - - - - - - - - - - *Get ready!* - - - - - - - - -

These words tell **how often** something happens.

~~usually~~   ~~rarely~~   often   sometimes   always
hardly ever   never   almost always

1 👥 **Work with a partner.
Write the words in the
correct places.**

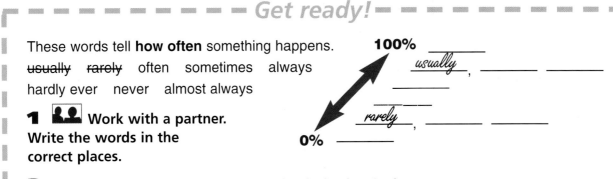

100% _____
usually , _____ _____
_____
_____ _____
rarely , _____
0% _____

2 For each word, find one thing you both do that is the same.
How many sentences can you write in five minutes?

We hardly ever write letters at work.
We often meet friends on Saturday.

Conversation 💬

We're always busy.

1 📻 **Listen.**

A

We're really busy today.
Is it always like this?

Yes, almost always.

Is it usually   Yes, it is.
How often is it   Every Friday.

B

What about our morning break?

We're usually too
busy to take one.

When is our   Sometimes it's
Do we get a   It's often

C

Really? I hope we never
miss our lunch break!

Well ... sometimes we
only get a short one.

always get   usually
usually have   most of the time

D

And we don't usually
have an afternoon
break, right?

Sure, we do. At
5 o'clock ... when
the office closes!

hardly ever   we go home
never   we finish work

Pronunciation focus

2 📻 **Listen again. Say the sentences. Match the stress and rhythm.**

3 👥 **Practice the conversation with a partner.
Then close your book. Have a conversation like this one.**

Listening 🔊

What's your job like?

1 🔊 Listen. Who is speaking? Number the pictures 1-4. There is one extra.

☐ **a hotel clerk**

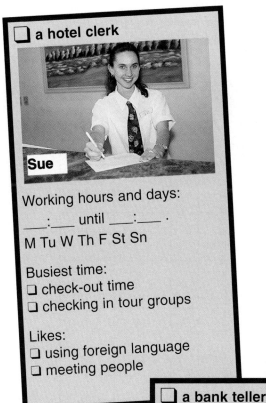

Sue

Working hours and days:
___:___ until ___:___ .
M Tu W Th F St Sn

Busiest time:
☐ check-out time
☐ checking in tour groups

Likes:
☐ using foreign language
☐ meeting people

1 **a secretary**

Linda

Working hours and days:
___:___ until ___:___ .
M Tu W Th F St Sn

Busiest time:
☐ Monday morning
☐ Friday afternoon

Dislikes:
☐ being under pressure
☐ filing

☐ **an airline ticket agent**

Sofia

Working hours and days:
___:___ until ___:___ .
M Tu W Th F St Sn

Busiest time:
☐ holidays
☐ weekends

Likes:
☐ flying
☐ meeting and helping people

☐ **a bank teller**

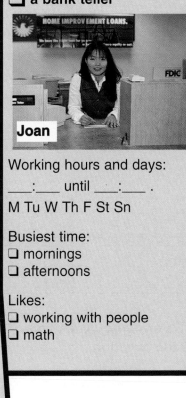

Joan

Working hours and days:
___:___ until ___:___ .
M Tu W Th F St Sn

Busiest time:
☐ mornings
☐ afternoons

Likes:
☐ working with people
☐ math

☐ **a tour guide**

Mari

Working schedule:
☐ almost always works weekends
☐ hardly ever works weekends

Busiest time:
☐ preparing for tours
☐ giving tours

Dislikes:
☐ tourists who complain
☐ office work

2 🔊 Listen. Write the times they work. Circle the days. Check (✔) the other answers.

Pair Work A
How often?

Student B, use activity file 43 (page 96).

1 Read the questions. Check (✔) the answers for yourself.

How often do you...	You						B					
	always	usually/almost always	often	sometimes	hardly ever/rarely	never	always	usually/almost always	often	sometimes	hardly ever/rarely	never
work or study on weekends?												
get to work or school late?												
have a coffee break in the morning?												
speak to foreigners at work or school?												
get tired at work or school?												
read something in English?												
go to meetings on ____day? (Write a day)												
have free-time at work or school?												

Write two more questions.

2 Ask B the questions. Check (✔) B's answers. When you and B have the same answer, circle the question.

How often do you work on weekends? I usually / hardly ever do.

┌ ─ ─ *Keep going!* ─ ─ ─ ─ ─ ➤

⬇ **3** Find at least five things B does more often than you. Find at least five things you do more often than B.

Writing Right 🖎

Memos

Memos are notes to other people in the same office.

1 Look at the memo
and the hints.

> ## MEMO
>
> TO: Frank Jordan
> FROM: Maki Ito
> DATE: July 8,(year)
> SUBJECT: New software
>
> The new computer software will be installed next
> Thursday. A training session will be

> *Remember!*
> ■ **To:**   Usually no address,
>   just a name
> ■ **Subject:** Tells what the memo is
>   about. Sometimes this
>   is *Re:* (regarding)

2 Complete the memo. Use the words below and
the words and information in the Office Survey.

Getting to work   Cindy Diaz   June 15, (year)
Ken Lawson   get to   come
drive   walk   take

???? Office Survey ????

How do you get to work?

	Always	Sometimes	Never
By bus	10	5	5
By car	8	8	4
On foot	2	1	17

> ## MEMO
>
> TO: *Cindy Diaz* _____
> FROM: _____
> DATE: _____
> SUBJECT: _____
>
> To help us plan for the new parking lot, I surveyed the
> staff. In our office, 10 people __*always*__ come by bus,
> _____ people sometimes _____ by bus but 5
> people _____ _____ the bus. As for driving, 8
> people always _____ _____ work by car and 8
> others _____ come by car. _____ people never
> _____ to work. Finally, only 2 people always
> _____ to work, _____ person sometimes comes on
> foot, but _____ people never walk to work.

Numbers 1.2.3.

1 🔊 Listen. Write the numbers you hear. Check by saying the numbers.

2 🔊 Listen. You will hear the numbers in sentences. Write only
the numbers. Check by saying them.

3 👥 Student A, use activity file 6 (page 83). Student B, use activity
file 25 (page 88).

7 Making appointments

Get ready!

Look at the different ways to say the time in English.

1 👥 **Work with a partner.**
Student A, use activity file 48 on page 100.
Student B, use activity file 55 on page 102.
Ask what time your partner does the things.
Say what time you do them. Who does
each thing first? Check (✔) the boxes.

EXAMPLE: A: What time do you get up?
B: At a quarter after 6.
A: I get up at 7.

It's __ (o'clock).

It's __ fifteen.
It's a quarter
after __.

It's __ thirty.
It's half past __.

It's __ forty-five.
It's a quarter
to __.

Conversation 💬

How about Tuesday afternoon?

1 📼 **Listen.**

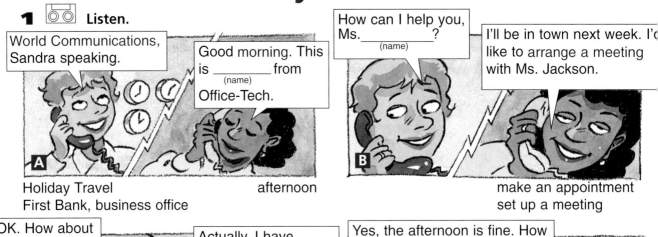

World Communications, Sandra speaking.

Good morning. This is _____ from (name) Office-Tech.

How can I help you, Ms. _____? (name)

I'll be in town next week. I'd like to arrange a meeting with Ms. Jackson.

Holiday Travel   afternoon
First Bank, business office

make an appointment
set up a meeting

OK. How about Tuesday morning?

Actually, I have another appointment then. Is Tuesday afternoon possible?

afternoon   morning

Yes, the afternoon is fine. How about 2:30? (Two-thirty)

2:30? Fine. I'll see you then. Thank you. Good-bye.

10:15 (ten-fifteen)   10:15 (a quarter after ten)
3:45 (three forty-five)   3:45 (a quarter to four)

Pronunciation focus

2 📼 **Listen again. Say the sentences. Match the stress and rhythm.**

3 👥 **Practice the conversation with a partner.**
Then close your book. Have a conversation like this one.

Listening 📻

When can we meet?

1 📻 **People are making and changing plans.**
Listen. Write the times and the plans.

1.

Thurs July 17

am *9:30 - 11:00 - meeting*
about new schedule

pm *1 - 2 - Meet Ms. Lee*
2 - Meet Mr. Carr
3:30 - Call Mr. Wilson

4.

Public Lecture

*Office Jobs
in the
next
10 years*

Dr. J. Wong

7:00 p.m. Tonight

2.

Tues 18

*Meeting with
Ms. Gray
3 p.m.*

Wed 19

5.

APA ✈ AsiaPacific Airways		
	Taipei	**Bangkok**
AP318	8:15 am	11:35 pm
AP307	5:20 pm	8:50 pm
	Tokyo	**Seoul**
AP304	10:30 am	12:50 pm
AP309	7:05 pm	9:25 pm

It's Culture

Starting times
The time a meeting starts can
depend on culture.
In English-speaking countries,
remember:

■ *Business meetings* usually
start on time. Get there a few
minutes early.

■ *Lunch or dinner.* Be there
on time.

■ *Parties.* Usually arrive a little
late.

Do meetings start on time in
your country?

3.

MEMO

*Meet Ms. Rivera for lunch.
_____ day at _____ .*

Group Work

Let's have lunch!

1 This is your pocket diary. Fill in everything you have planned the next week. Include classes, work, appointments, etc.

Mon. am ....

pm ....

Tues. am ....

pm ....

Wed. am ....

pm ....

Thurs. am ....

pm ....

Fri. am ....

pm ....

Sat. am ....

pm ....

Sun. am ....

pm ....

2 Work with a partner. Use the telephone to make an appointment.
Then change partners. Make five different appointments.

A: Hello.

B: Hello, this is (first and last name).
Is (first and last name) there?

A: Speaking.

B: Oh, hi (first name) .
I'm calling to ask if you'd like to (activity).

A: That sounds good. When?

B: How about (day and time)?

A: (repeat day and time)?
That sounds good.
(or) Sorry, I'm busy then.
How about (different day and time)?

B: OK. Let's plan on that.

A: See you then. Good-bye.

B: Bye.

Ideas

have lunch
study together
play tennis
do something special
(go to a movie, party, etc.)

─ ─ ─ Keep going! ─ ─ ─ ─ ➤

3 Try to make more appointments. Make as many as you can.

Writing Right ✎
Making an appointment

1 Look at Ms. Sousa's calendar. Read the letter. Write the missing dates.

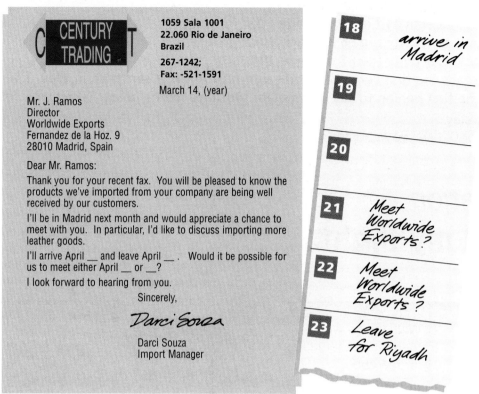

2 Mr. Ramos will be away on business on April 21 and 22. He wants to meet on April 20. Write a letter from Mr. Ramos to Ms. Souza. Follow this form:

1. *Acknowledge the letter:*
   Thank you for your letter of March 14.
2. *Explain why you can't meet when suggested:*
   Unfortunately, I will be ...
3. *Suggest a different date:*
   Would it be possible ...
4. *Close politely:*
   I am looking forward to seeing you next month.

Numbers 1.2.3.

1 📻 Listen. Write the times you hear by drawing hands on the clocks.

  a.   b.   c.   d.   e.   f.   g.

Check by saying the times.

2 📻 Listen. You will hear the numbers in sentences. Write only the numbers. Check by saying them.

3 👥 Student **A**, use activity file 7 (page 83). Student **B**, use activity 26 (page 88).

8 Recent experiences

- - - - - - *Get ready!* - - - - - - -

1 Work in groups of three.
Student A, look at activity file 49 on page 100.
Student B, look at activity file 56 on page 102.
Student C, look at activity file 62 on page 104.
One person reads the first verb. The other two race to say a sentence in the
past tense. The first person to say a complete sentence gets a point. Take turns.

EXAMPLE: A: stay.
B or C: I stayed at home..

Conversation

I missed my flight.

1 Listen.

Hong Kong	reserved the seat
Seoul	got the ticket

she	was late for check-in
	went at the wrong time

were late?	check-in was at 8 o'clock.
had the time wrong?	the flight left at 10.

another	there weren't any open seats
a different	it was overbooked

Pronunciation focus

2 Listen again. Say the sentences. Match the stress and rhythm.

3 Practice the conversation with a partner.
Then close your book. Have a conversation like this one.

Listening 📼
How did you get here?

1 📼 **Listen. Complete the chart. Which would you choose?
Check (✔) your answer.**

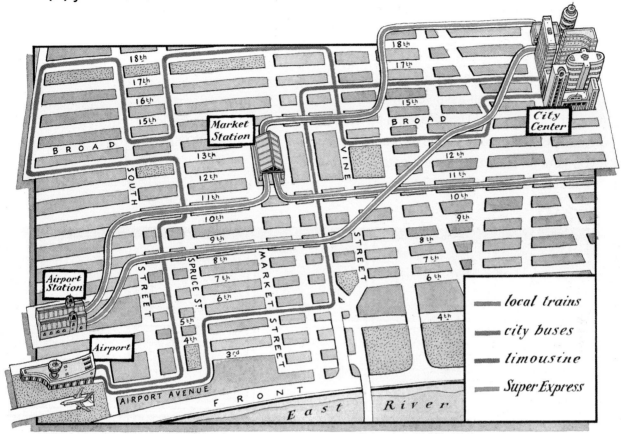

	Time	**Cost**	**How many each hour?**				
❑ local train	*1 hour*	*$8*	1	2	③	4	5
❑ city bus	_____	_____	1	2	3	4	5
❑ airport limousine	_____	_____	1	2	3	4	5
❑ Super Express	_____	_____	1	2	3	4	5

2 📼 **Paul is late. Listen. Check (✔) what happened.**

1. He ❑ had / ❑ forgot the directions.

2. He ❑ took / ❑ missed the Super Express.

3. He took ❑ a local train. / ❑ the airport limousine.

4. He ❑ didn't change / ❑ changed trains at Market Station.

5. He waited about ❑ an hour. / ❑ 30 minutes.

6. He took ❑ the wrong train. / ❑ a taxi.

7. He went ❑ to Market Station. / ❑ back to the airport.

Paul

Group Work

Business and pleasure

1 Imagine that you took a trip in South East Asia. After you finished working, you had a vacation. Play the game in groups of four.

- Use one book for the game board. Each player puts a marker (a coin, eraser, etc.) on the "start" space.
- Roll a die. Move that many spaces. If you don't have a die, use activity file 68 on page 106.
- The player to your left asks you the question.
- Answer the question. Use the hints [in **bold**] or think of your own answer. You get 2 points for each answer.
- If you land on a Penalty space, you lose 2 points.
- The first person to get 10 points wins.

> I was in Hong Kong.

START

Where were you last week? **[be/ in Hong Kong]** →	How did you get there? **[fly/ on United]** →	Where did you stay? **[stay/ at the Hilton]** →	Who did you meet? **[meet/ Mr. Lee]** →	PENALTY! You didn't bring some important papers ↓
What did you do at the bank? **[change/ some money]** ↓ $>¥>£	What did you do in the morning? **[make/ an appointment]** ←	PENALTY! You didn't call the office. ←	How long did the flight take? **[take/ 3 hours]** ←	Where did you go next? **[go/ to Singapore]** ←
PENALTY! You didn't have the new brochures. →	How did you get to your meeting? **[go/ by bus]** →	PENALTY! You were late for the meeting. →	Why were you late for the meeting? **[get off/ at wrong bus stop]** →	Where did you leave the map? **[leave/ in my hotel room]** ↓
PENALTY! The hotel lost your reservation.	What happened at the airport? **[I/ check in/ late]** ←	What did you do next?\ **[go to Bangkok/ for a vacation]** ←	What did you see? **[see/ our new office]** ←	When did the meeting finish? **[finish/ about 4:30]** ←
What did you do in Bangkok? **[buy/ lots of souvenirs]** →	PENALTY! You spent too much money. →	Did you go on a city tour? **[no/ arrive/ late]** →	Did you take a bus? **[no/ rent/ a car]** →	What did you do on the beach? **[write/ some postcards]** ↓
That was fast! If you don't have 10 points, start again. ↱	PENALTY! They lost your suitcase. ←	What happened then? **[fly home/ one day late]** ←	PENALTY! You forgot to reconfirm your flight. ←	How did you get to the airport? **[take/ a taxi]** ←

- - Keep going!- - - - ➤

2 Play again. This time, tell about a real trip you have taken. If a question is about something you didn't do, your partner can ask a different question.

Writing Right ✎

Complete the memo

1 Complete Kevin's memo to his manager.
Write the past forms of these verbs:

are ~~arrive~~ cancel check do not
finish forget go have is make meet
return see talk

2 Now write about a trip you took.

- Where did you go?
- How long did you stay?
- How did you get there? Where did you stay?
- What did you do?
- Did you have any problems?

Use at least eight past tense verbs.

MEMO

TO: Julia Martin
FROM: Kevin Ikeda
DATE: July 12, (year)
RE: Trip to San Francisco

Monday, July 10th

I _arrived_ in San Francisco at 10 a.m. After
I _____ in at the Plaza Hotel, I
_____ Ms. Lee of Century Trading for
lunch. We _____ for 2 hours and then we
_____ Mr. Cara. We _____ a good
meeting, but there _____ two small
problems. I _____ some schedules and he
_____ have the new brochures.

Tuesday, July 11th

At Union Bank, Mr. Wilson _____ very
busy, so he _____ our meeting. I
_____ another appointment with him for
next week. Then I _____ to our local
office and _____ some reports.
I _____ to Los Angeles in the afternoon.

Numbers 1, 2, 3.

1 Find the time zone you live in. Write O in the box.
Write +1, +2, +3, etc. in the boxes to the right of your zone.
Write –1, –2, –3, etc. in the boxes to the left of your zone.

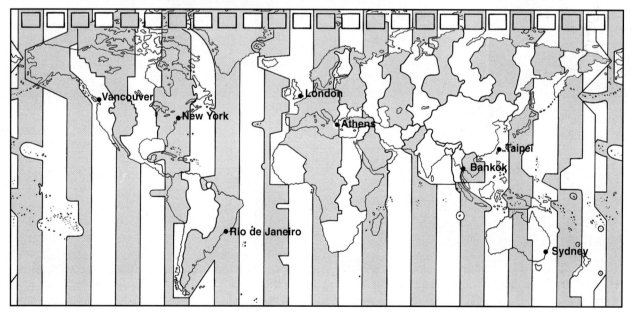

2 🔊 Listen. What time is it in these cities right now? Find the cities.
Add (+) or subtract (–) the number of hours you wrote in the boxes.
Write the times.

3 👥 Student A, use activity file 8 (page 83). Student B, use activity file 27 (page 88).

9 Locations

— — — — — — — — — *Get ready!* — — — — — — — —

1 🧑‍🤝‍🧑 **Work with a partner. Look at the picture. Write these words in the correct places:**

~~on~~   under   to the right of   to the left of
~~between~~   in front of   in back of   in

2 👥 **Now work in groups of four. Each person puts four small objects on a desk. Use things like keys, pens, coins, etc. Three people close their eyes. The other person moves two things. Partners, look. Who can be the first to find the changes?**

EXAMPLE:
The scissors were on the book.
Now they're between the ruler and the pencil.

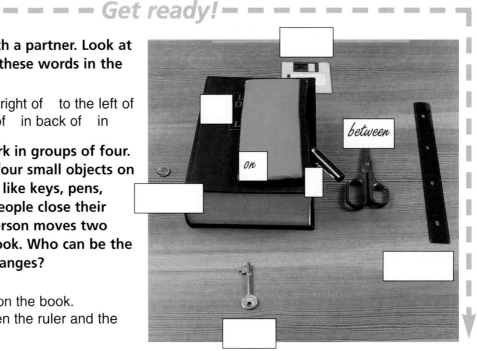

Conversation 🗩

Where's the restaurant?

1 📻 **Listen.**

A
Excuse me? Where's the restaurant in the hotel?
There are two ma'am.

three
several

B
Really?
There's a Chinese Restaurant on the fifth floor.

I see.   next to the front door.
Are there?   in the basement.

C
On the fifth floor?
Yes, ma'am. There's also a garden restaurant. It's on the roof.

Next to the front door?   in back of the hotel
In the basement?   next to the main building

D
On the roof?
That's right. The weather's beautiful today. I'm sure you'll enjoy it.

In the back?   tonight
By the main building?   this evening

Pronunciation focus

2 📻 **Listen again. Say the sentences. Match the stress and rhythm.**

3 🧑‍🤝‍🧑 **Practice the conversation with a partner. Then close your book. Have a conversation like this one.**

Listening 📼
That's wrong!

1 This is a travel agency. Look at the picture for exactly one minute. Try to remember everything in the picture. Be sure to notice where the people and things are.

2 📼 Close your book. Listen. Someone is describing the picture. The speaker makes some mistakes. On a piece of paper, write the mistakes.

3 📼 Listen again. Circle the speaker's mistakes on the picture.

Pair Work A 👥

Where can I find it?

Student B, use activity file 44 (page 97).

1 Look at the hotel. Ask B where these places are:

- the newsstand
- the gym (gymnasium)
- the tennis courts
- the lounge
- the Chinese restaurant
- the business center

Write the words in the correct place.

2 Answer B's questions.

EXAMPLE:
Where's the conference room?
It's on the second floor.
It's to the right of the elevator.
The conference room is across from the gift shop.

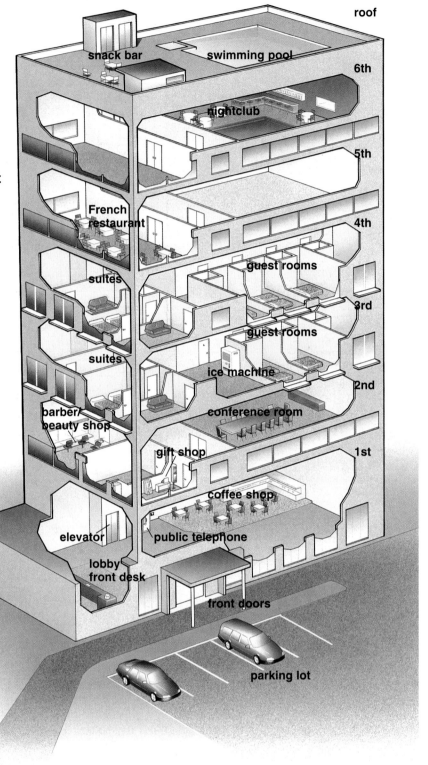

3 Describe the place where you work or your room at home. B, draw a picture of it. When you don't understand something, ask. Was the picture correct?

Writing Right

Leaving notes

1 People are meeting at the Grand Hotel. Read the notes. Where will the people meet? Write the numbers in the circles.

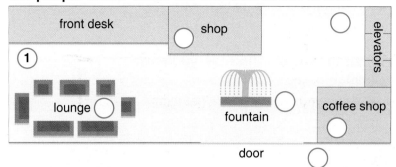

1.
> **The Grand Hotel**   **Message**
>
> Name: *Mr. Andre da Silva* Room number: *2943*
>
> *Mr. Lopez will be here at 11:30.*
> *He'll meet you by the front desk.*
> *A. Souza*

4.
> **The Grand Hotel**   **Message**
>
> Name: *Jim Wilson*   Room number: *1227*
>
> *Hope you had a good flight.*
> *Let's meet tomorrow morning*
> *at 10:00. I'll be by the*
> *fountain. – Chuck*

2.
> **The Grand Hotel**   **Message**
>
> Name: *Mr. Cameron* Room number: *812*
>
> *We leave for the conference*
> *at 8:15. I'll wait for you*
> *by the elevators. Chris Emil*

5.
> **The Grand Hotel**   **Message**
>
> Name: *Ms. R. Rossi* Room number: *607*
>
> *Mr. Lane called. He'll*
> *wait for you in the*
> *lounge at 5:00.*

3.
> **The Grand Hotel**   **Message**
>
> Name: *Ms. H.S. Chung* Room number: *1620*
>
> *The meeting starts at 10:30.*
> *I'll pick you up in front*
> *of the hotel at 9:45.*
> *T. Kato*

6.
> **The Grand Hotel**   **Message**
>
> Name: *Janet Archer* Room number: *736*
>
> *Janet,*
> *I went out this morning.*
> *Let's meet in the coffee shop.*
> *Terri*

2 You are meeting people at work, school or well-known places. Write three notes telling where and when to meet.

Numbers 1, 2, 3.

1 Listen. Write the numbers you hear. Check by saying the numbers.

2 Listen. You will hear the numbers in sentences. Write only the numbers. Check by saying them.

3 Student A, use activity file 9 (page 84). Student B, use activity file 28 (page 89).

Review, UNITS 1-9

1 👥 Work with a partner. This is a speaking contest. You will see how long you can speak in English. Your turn is over when you:
- stop for five seconds.
- say a word that is not English.

Partner, listen. Time the speaker. When the speaker finishes, you must ask at least three questions. Then change parts.

Your topic: Think about your job **or** imagine you have a job. What things do you do every day?

Find the mistakes

2 👥 Work with a partner. Look at these sentences. Each sentence has a mistake. Find the mistakes. Correct them.

3 📼 Now listen. Are you right? If you are correct, check (✔) OK. If your answer is wrong, fix it. Then look at the page in parentheses. Find a correct example.

1. ~~What~~ *How* do you say that in English?   (page 11)

2. She fly to Brazil last week.   ❑ OK (page 36)

3. The swimming pool is in the roof.   ❑ OK (page 38)

4. A flight attendant gets higher pay a travel agent.   ❑ OK (page 15)

5. Being an office worker is more dangerous than being a police officer.   ❑ OK (page 15)

6. The meeting starts at nine-thirty o'clock.   ❑ OK (page 30)

7. What do you spell it?   ❑ OK (page 11)

8. Friday is our busiest day. We're almost busy then.   ❑ OK (page 26)

9. Do you can speak English?   ❑ OK (page 20)

10. I'd like to make a meeting with Ms. Lima.   ❑ OK (page 30)

There are some other ways to correct the sentences. If you think your answer is right, ask your teacher.

Talking tasks

4 👥 Work with a partner.
Student A, look at the talking task cards in activity file 19 (page 86).
Student B, look at the talking task cards in activity file 38 (page 91).

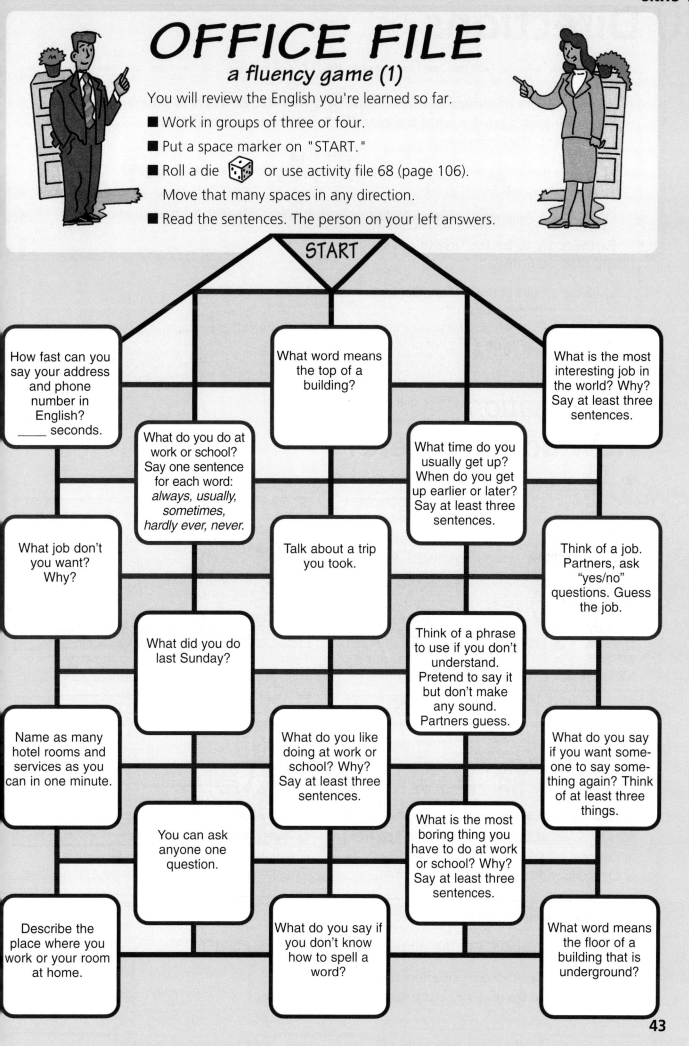

OFFICE FILE
a fluency game (1)

You will review the English you're learned so far.

■ Work in groups of three or four.

■ Put a space marker on "START."

■ Roll a die or use activity file 68 (page 106). Move that many spaces in any direction.

■ Read the sentences. The person on your left answers.

START

How fast can you say your address and phone number in English? ____ seconds.

What word means the top of a building?

What is the most interesting job in the world? Why? Say at least three sentences.

What do you do at work or school? Say one sentence for each word: *always, usually, sometimes, hardly ever, never.*

What time do you usually get up? When do you get up earlier or later? Say at least three sentences.

What job don't you want? Why?

Talk about a trip you took.

Think of a job. Partners, ask "yes/no" questions. Guess the job.

What did you do last Sunday?

Think of a phrase to use if you don't understand. Pretend to say it but don't make any sound. Partners guess.

Name as many hotel rooms and services as you can in one minute.

What do you like doing at work or school? Why? Say at least three sentences.

What do you say if you want some-one to say some-thing again? Think of at least three things.

You can ask anyone one question.

What is the most boring thing you have to do at work or school? Why? Say at least three sentences.

Describe the place where you work or your room at home.

What do you say if you don't know how to spell a word?

What word means the floor of a building that is underground?

10 Directions

- - - - - - - - - - - - *Get ready!* - - - - - - - - - - - - -

1 **Work in groups of three. Think of a well-known place in your area. Don't tell your partners what the place is. Tell them how to get there. Use some of these phrases:**

Go straight Turn right Turn left Go down/Take (that street) Go past (that building)

Partners, try to be the first to guess the place. Continue.

EXAMPLE: Start at the station. Go east three blocks.
Turn left. Go past the bank.
You'll see it in front of you.

Remember!

Don't use "you" with directions or instructions.
"Go straight." not "~~You~~ go straight."

Conversation 🗩

How do I get there?

1 🔊 **Listen.**

I need to go to City Bank. How do I get there?

City Bank? Turn left when you leave the office.

Which way is it?   Make a left (turn)
Where is it?   Go left

OK.

Then go straight on that street for two blocks.

I see.   until you get to the post office
All right.   until you come to a traffic light

Let's see. Turn left and go two blocks.

That's right.

to the post office   That's it.
to the traffic light   Yes.

And then?

City Bank is across the street, on the corner.

Thank you.

Thank you very much.   on the right
Thanks a lot.   next to a bookstore

Pronunciation focus

2 🔊 Listen again. Say the sentences. Match the stress and rhythm.

3 Practice the conversation with a partner.
Then close your book. Have a conversation like this one.

Listening 📼

Which way is it?

1 📼 **Start at at the bottom of the map each time. Listen. Follow the directions. Write the number on the correct buildings.**

1. Century Trading
2. Horizon Travel
3. The Plaza Hotel

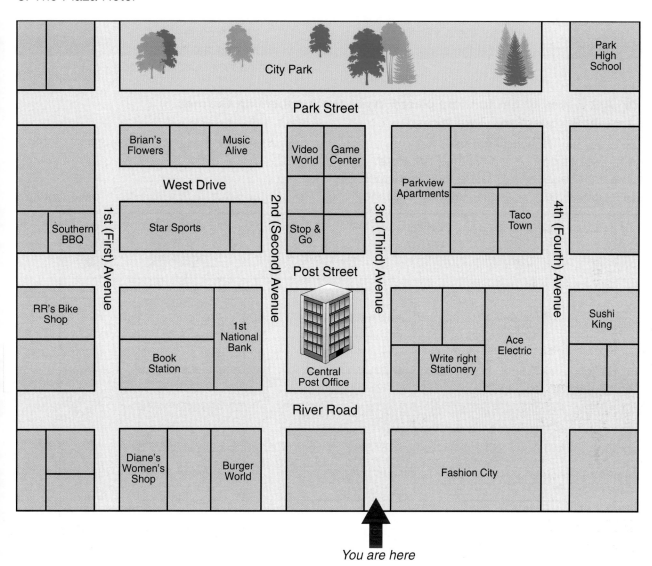

You are here

2 📼 **Listen again. Number the directions (1-4) in the boxes.**

1. ❏ turn right
   ☑ go to the corner
   ❏ go straight
   ❏ turn left

2. ❏ go past the Post Office
   ❏ turn right at the next corner
   ❏ it's in the middle of the block
   ❏ turn left

3. ❏ turn left on West Drive
   ❏ turn left on River Road
   ❏ cross the street
   ❏ turn right

Pair Work A

Turn right and then...

Student B, use activity file 45 (page 98).

Go down Take	this street 6th Street	to	8th Street. the corner of 6th and Broadway.
Go past	the bookstore.	Go	straight to the second street. north to the park.
Turn	right (at the bookstore). left (at the second street).	It's	on the corner. next to the hotel. the first building on the right.

1 Ask B how to get to these places. Write the numbers on the map.
Answer B's questions. Take turns.

Excuse me. How do I get to ... ?

1. a post office   7. the Park Hotel
3. a travel agency   9. a stationery store
5. a bookstore   11. the Sun Building

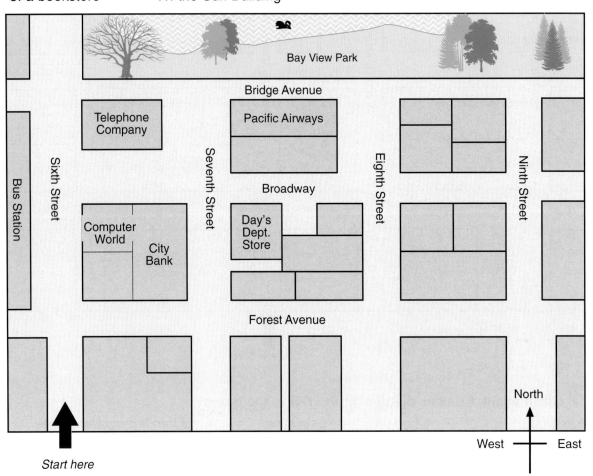

Start here

--- *Keep going!* - - - - - ➤

2 What are the best places in your area for a tourist to visit?
Think of at least five places. Tell B. Listen to B's ideas. Together,
decide the six best places. Write directions to each one.

Writing Right 🖎
Getting to the office

1 Follow the arrows (→) on the map. Put the directions in order.

___ You'll see the Bank of Canada on the corner.

_1_ When you leave the bus station, cross the street directly in front of you.

___ After you cross Denny Street, go past the hotel to the corner of Bridge and Howe.

___ Turn right and then go down Pacific for two blocks.

___ Turn left at the bank and then go straight.

___ Turn left onto Howe and our office is around the corner, next to the Ocean Hotel.

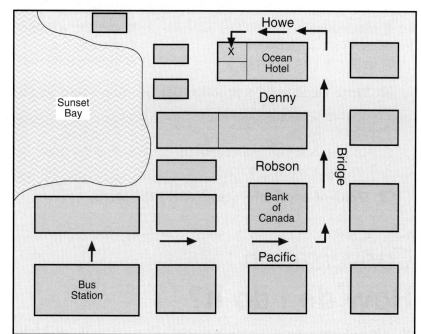

2 Now, write a letter to Ms. Janet Kane. Her address is 830 Beach Road, San Diego, California 94750. Tell her how to get to your office or school. Use a business letter format (see page 9).

Start with:
Thank you for your telephone call yesterday. Here are the directions to our office (school).
When you leave (the station, airport, bus, etc.)

End with:
We look forward to seeing you next month.

Numbers 1.2.3.

Listen to the examples:
EXAMPLES: 41st   2nd   23rd   9th

1 🔘🔘 Listen. Write the numbers you hear. Use *st, nd, rd* and *th*.
Check by saying the numbers.

2 🔘🔘 Listen. You will hear the numbers in sentences. Write only the numbers. Check by saying them.

3 👥 Student A, use activity file 10 (page 84). Student B, use activity file 29 (page 89).

11 Describing processes

- - - - - - - - - - Get ready! - - - - - - - - - -

1 👥 **Work with a partner. Choose one of these processes:**

- ▇ making tea
- ▇ using a pay phone
- ▇ getting on an airplane

- ▇ sending a letter
- ▇ starting a car
- ▇ getting dressed

2 Write steps for the process. Use as many steps as possible.

EXAMPLE: Opening a door

1. Walk to the door.
2. Put your hand on the doorknob.
3. Turn the knob to the right.

4. Step back.
5. Pull the door.

3 Think of another process. Write the steps.

Conversation 💬

How do I do it?

1 📟 **Listen.**

afternoon

| need to do | fill this out |
| do | complete this form |

And after that?   Now
Now what?   Next

Is there anything else?   get
Am I finished?   prepare

Pronunciation focus

2 📟 **Listen again. Say the sentences. Match the stress and rhythm.**

3 👥 **Practice the conversation with a partner.**
Then close your book. Have a conversation like this one.

Listening 🔊

Buying traveler's checks

James is going on a business trip. He needs to buy traveler's checks.
He's never bought them from a machine before.

1 🔊 **Listen. Number the pictures 1–5.**

2 🔊 **Listen again. What words are used for each instruction? Write the missing words.**

1. First, _____ the language you want.

2. _____ the screen for the one you want.

3. _____ OK.

4. Next, _____ the correct amount of money.

5. Finally, _____ all of the checks.

It's Culture

Please

Some languages use a word like "please" for instructions:

Please press this button.

This is unusual in English. Use "please" for something that helps you:

Please call me.

Don't use it for something that helps the other person.

Do you use a word like "please" to give instructions in your country?

Group Work 👥

How does it work?

Work in groups of three.
Student A, use activity file 50 on page 100.
Student B, use activity file 57 on page 102.
Student C, use activity file 64 on page 105.

1 Put one book on the table. Look at the pictures. Read one set of
instructions. Read them one step at a time. Partners, listen. Say the
name of the process. The first person to say the process gets one point.

electronic translator	airport check-in	photocopier	cassette recorder
computer printer	phone card	answering machine	calculator
electronic typewriter	bank draft	a vending machine	a fax machine
changing money	computer	passport control	hotel check-in
VCR (video cassette recorder)	bank card	compact disk (CD) player	cashing traveler's checks

2 Think of machines you know how to use and processes you do.
Pantomime them. Partners, guess what the person is doing.
Say the steps in the process:

First..., After that...

Writing Right ✍

Using a fax machine

1 Look at the pictures. Read the instructions. Write the missing verbs:

adjust   enter   pick up
~~place~~   press   send
take out

If there are any words you don't know, skip them. Do the other steps. Then, try to guess the meaning.

2 Now, think of a machine you know how to use. Write the instructions. Your instructions must have at least five steps.

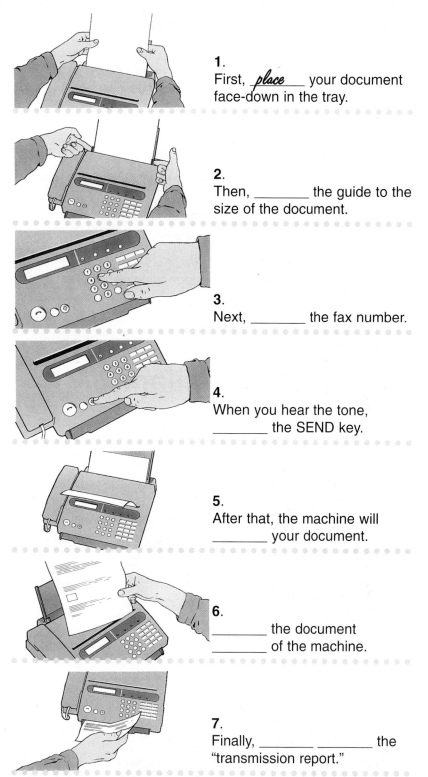

1.
First, _place_ your document face-down in the tray.

2.
Then, _____ the guide to the size of the document.

3.
Next, _____ the fax number.

4.
When you hear the tone, _____ the SEND key.

5.
After that, the machine will _____ your document.

6.
_____ the document _____ of the machine.

7.
Finally, _____ _____ the "transmission report."

Numbers 1, 2, 3,

1 📼 Listen to the examples:

EXAMPLES: 15.2   0.94   21.03   104.78

Listen. Write the numbers you hear. Check by saying the numbers.

2 📼 Listen. You will hear the numbers in sentences. Write only the numbers. Check by saying them.

3 👥 Student A, use activity file 11 (page 84). Student B, use activity file 30 (page 89).

For decimals (.), say "point." 2.1 is "two point one."

12 Stating preferences

- - - - - - - - - - - Get ready!- - - - - - - - - - -

1 Find someone who can say "yes" to each question below. Write that persons name next to the question. Use each name only one time.

Do you like...

- restaurants better than clubs? _____
- office work better than meeting people? _____
- nature more than cities? _____
- the beach more than shopping? _____
- busy days more than boring days? _____
- computers more than typewriters? _____
- relaxing vacations more than exciting vacations? _____
- writing letters better than telephoning people. _____

Conversation

How about Thailand?

1 Listen.

interesting, with an excellent hotel
exciting, with good shopping

I've been there
Hong Kong's too crowded

more exotic   exciting
less crowded   much better

one or two weeks   the two week tour
at a first class or   first class
a budget hotel   budget

Pronunciation focus

2 Listen again. Say the sentences. Match the stress and rhythm.

3 Practice the conversation with a partner.
Then close your book. Have a conversation like this one.

Listening 📼

What kind of vacation do you like?

1 What kind of vacation do you like? When you travel, are these things important to you? Mark your preferences in the boxes.

✔ = very important   X = less important

☐ relaxing   ☐ good restaurants   ☐ nightlife (music, dancing, etc.)

☐ sports facilities   ☐ nature   ☐ cultural events (theater, art, etc.)

☐ shopping   ☐ a good hotel   ☐ sightseeing tours

2 📼 Listen. What do these people like? Mark their preferences (✔ or X) in the boxes.

1.

James

☐ restaurants   ☐ nightlife
☐ sightseeing   ☐ nature
☐ shopping

2.

Eri

☐ relaxing   ☐ sightseeing
☐ nature   ☐ nightlife
☐ a good hotel

3.

Lee

☐ excitement   ☐ nightlife
☐ a good hotel   ☐ sightseeing
☐ restaurants

4.

Alberto

☐ nightlife   ☐ sport facilities
☐ cultural events   ☐ restaurants
☐ shopping

Group Work 👥👥
Mystic Island Tours

Half the students are customers. Customers, use this page.
Half are travel agents. Travel agents, count off by threes (1–2–3, 1–2–3, etc.)
Travel agent 1, use activity file 51, (page 101).
Travel agent 2, use activity file 58, (page 103).
Travel agent 3, use activity file 66, (page 105).

Does the hotel have	a swimming pool? restaurants? air-conditioning?	Yes, it does. No, it doesn't.
Where is the hotel located?		It's on the beach.
How far is it from the town center?		It's only a 15 minute walk.
Are	meals tours included (in the package)?	Yes, breakfast is included. No, they aren't included.
How much does the tour cost?		Two thousand dollars including air-fare.

1 Customers: You have two weeks for your vacation. You are going to Mystic Island. You must choose your tour package.
Talk to the agents. Fill in the chart.

When you decide the tour you want, circle it.

Travel agencies:	HORIZON		Sunshine		WORLD TRAVEL	
	Yes	No	Yes	No	Yes	No
Hotel Facilities						
swimming pool	❏	❏	❏	❏	❏	❏
restaurants	❏	❏	❏	❏	❏	❏
bar/night club	❏	❏	❏	❏	❏	❏
Meals included						
breakfast	❏	❏	❏	❏	❏	❏
lunch	❏	❏	❏	❏	❏	❏
dinner	❏	❏	❏	❏	❏	❏
Tours Included	❏	❏	❏	❏	❏	❏
Location						
beach	❏	❏	❏	❏	❏	❏
town center	❏	❏	❏	❏	❏	❏
market	❏	❏				
Price:	$		$		$	

┌ ─ ─ *Keep going!* ─ ─ ─ ➡

2 Change parts. Travel agents become customers. Customers become agents. Imagine a tour to a famous place in your country. Where will customers stay? What will people do? How much will the tour cost? Agents, try to "sell" your tour.

Writing Right
Making a reservation

1 Read this fax. Fill out the hotel reservation form.

FAX MESSAGE

Attention: Hotel La Blanca
Reservation Department
From: Jean Wallace
Date: October 18, (year)
Re: Room reservation
Total pages including this one: 1

HORIZON
TRAVEL
10 Bank Street
White Plains
New York 10605
Phone: (914) 993-5000
Fax: (914) 997-8115

If you do not receive all pages, please contact us immediately

Please confirm one (1) double room.
December 28 to January 2 (5 nights).
Guest: Mr. Dan M. Lennox.
Charge: SuccessCard 934 243 132342
Please also confirm rate of
US$125 per night.

Hotel La Blanca
Concepción, Chile

Guest's name ___ last ___ first ___ middle initial

Check in ___ / ___ Check out ___ / ___

Room type: ___ Room rate: ___

Payment ___

Travel Agent ___ Agent's fax number ___

2 Now, write a fax reserving a single hotel room for your teacher.
Check in is next Friday. Check out is Sunday.

Numbers 1.2.3.

1 🔊 Listen. Write the different ways to say $147.25.
Write in words, not numbers:

One hundred and forty-seven dollars and twenty-five cents.

2 🔊 Listen. Now write the amounts and prices.
Write in numbers. Check by saying them.

3 👥 Student A, use activity file 12 (page 84).
Student B, use activity file 31 (page 89).

1 (hundred, thousand,...) can be "a": a hundred, a thousand...

13 Current activities

Get ready!

👥 **Work in groups of three.**
Student A, look at activity file 52 on page 101.
Student B, look at activity file 59 on page 103.
Student C, look at activity file 65 on page 105.

1 One person pantomimes an action.
Partners, guess what that person is doing. Take turns.

EXAMPLE:

A:

B or C: Are you sitting in the sun?

If you don't know the word in English, ask:
How do you say _____ in English?

Conversation 💬

The meeting is starting.

1 📻 Listen.

Let's go. The meeting is starting.

Now? But it usually starts at 1:30.

beginning

in the afternoon
later

We're discussing the report.

Oh, that's right! Is everyone there?

The boss is giving a
We're having a special

I forgot
of course

Almost everyone. The secretaries are still printing the copies.

I'm coming right now.

finishing
getting

leaving right away
on my way

Remember!

■ Use the *simple present* for things that usually happen:
I write reports a lot.

■ Use *present continuous* (*be* + verb + *ing*) for things happening now:
I'm writing the report now.

Pronunciation focus

2 📻 Listen again. Say the sentences. Match the stress and rhythm.

3 👥 Practice the conversation with a partner.
Then close your book. Have a conversation like this one.

Listening 🔲

I think he's using a computer.

1 Work with a partner. Look at the pictures. What do you think these people are doing? Write your answers. Use the *-ing* form of the verbs.

1.

I think he's *reading something* .
❑ yes   No, he's really _____ .
Extra information: *finish in 10 minutes* .

4.

Maybe she's _____ .
❑ yes   No, she's really _____ .
Extra information: _____ .

2.

Maybe she's _____ .
❑ yes   No, she's _____ .
Extra information: _____ .

5.

Maybe they're _____ .
❑ yes   No, they're _____ .
Extra information: _____ .

3.

I guess he's _____ .
❑ yes   No, actually he's _____ .
Extra information: _____ .

2 🔲 Listen. Were you right? Check (✔) yes. If you were wrong, write the correct answer. Write one more piece of information for each picture.

Pair Work A
Find the differences.

Student B, use activity file 46 (page 99).

1 B's picture is a little different than yours.
What are the people doing? Ask about B's picture. Tell about your picture.
Find the differences. Circle them.

A: What's Ms. Shaw doing?
B: She's waiting in line.
A: In my picture, she's checking in.

A: Is Karen checking in?
B: No, she's waiting in line.

- - - Keep going! - - - - ➡

2 A, look around the room for one minute. Try to remember what everyone
is doing. Then close your eyes.
B, say what people are doing. Say four sentences. One sentence is wrong.
A, try to find the "mistake." Then change parts. Continue.

Ms. Wade is standing in the back of the room.
Tanya is talking to Roberto.
Ken is asking a question.
Ruth is writing something.

Writing Right ✍

I'm checking on them now.

1 Read the fax. Is the writer ❑ thanking someone, ❑ apologizing or ❑ making an appointment? Check (✔) your answer.

FAX

To: Maki Ito, World Travel
From: Roy Green, Intertech Software
Date 10/29
Re: Your fax of 10/25

Total page including this one: 1

Intertech
SOFTWARE
Phone: (206) 555-2378
Fax: (206) 555-3894

Dear Maki,

Thanks for your fax of Oct. 25. Sorry I didn't respond earlier. I'm very busy because we're moving[1] into a new office next week. I'm writing[2] letters, packing[3] boxes, and talking[4] to customers all at the same time!

Anyway, to answer one of the questions in your fax, the Los Angeles office opens[5] at ten a.m. It closes[6] at five but someone always stays[7] until six or seven.

Concerning the late reports, I'm checking[8] on them now. It usually only takes[9] two or three days to get them.

Finally, I'm getting[10] the rest of the information you need this afternoon. I'll send it right away.

Again, I apologize for the delays.

Sincerely,

Roy Green

Roy Green

> **Remember!**
>
> You can also use *be + verb + ing* for the future.
> I'm writing the report tomorrow.

Look at the verbs (1-10). Do they refer to usual or regular actions (U), actions now (N) or future actions (F)? Write U, N or F for each.

1. _____   3. _____   5. _____   7. _____   9. _____
2. _____   4. _____   6. _____   8. _____   10. _____

2 Now, write about this week. Include:
- ▪ at least three things you usually do (U)
- ▪ at least three things you're doing right now (N)
- ▪ at least three things you're doing later this week (F)

When you finish, underline the verbs.

Numbers 1.2.3.

1 📼 Listen. Write the letters and numbers you hear. Check by saying the letters and numbers.

2 📼 Listen. You will hear letters and numbers in sentences. Write only the letters and numbers. Check by saying them.

3 👥 Student A, use activity file 13 (page 85). Student B, use activity file 32 (page 90).

14 Using the telephone

--- Get ready! ---

1 Stand up. Find a partner. Stand back-to-back. You are calling directory assistance. Ask for your partner's phone number. Write it. Then change partners. Write as many phone numbers as you can write in five minutes. Use this conversation:

A: Directory assistance. May I help you?
B: I'd like the number for (A's name)*.
A: Just a moment, please.
   That number is (use your own phone number or make one up).
B: (Say the number again to check.)
A: That's right.
B: Thank you. Goodbye.
A: Goodbye.

Remember!

■ When saying telephone numbers, zero is pronounced "oh."
■ Don't say anything for the hyphen (-). Just pause.

Conversation 💬

May I help you?

1 📻 Listen.

First National Bank. May I help you?

This is _____ from Southern Star Services. Is Ms. Martin there? (name)

Horizon Travel.
Interlink.

May I speak to Ms. Martin?
Is Ms. Martin in?

I'm sorry. She's in a meeting right now. May I take a message.

Yes, could you ask her to call me back?

not available now
not at her desk

tell her to
have her

I'd be happy to. Does she have your number?

It's 555-0477.

Could you give me
May I have

555-0477? And could you spell your name, please?

tell her
let her know

It's C A R T E R.

Thank you. I'll give her the message. Good-bye.

Pronunciation focus

2 📻 Listen again. Say the sentences. Match the stress and rhythm.

3 👥 Practice the conversation with a partner.
Then close your book. Have a conversation like this one.

Listening 🔊

May I take a message?

1 🔊 **Listen. Write the messages.**

1.

To: *J. Yagi*

While you were out

Mr. *Scott Jordan*
Ms.

of *Pineapple Computers* called

☐ will call back.

☐ return the call:

Number: _____

4.

To: *Robert Watts*

While you were out

Mr. _____
Ms.

of _____ called.

☐ will call back.

☐ return the call:

Number: _____

Message:

2.

MESSAGE

Pat,
Joanne called.
She said _____

_____

_____

3.

Paulo Lima called.
_____
_____
_____

It's Culture

When you telephone

Say your name and company **before** you say who you want to talk to:

"This is **(your name)** from **(company)**. Is **(the other person's name)** there?"

When do you say your name when you telephone in your country?

Pair Work A

May I speak to...

Student B, use activity file 69 (page 107).

1 You and B will have eight telephone conversations.
Sit back-to-back so you can't see each other. Read each card.
Cards 1, 3, 5, 7 = A calls B. Cards 2, 4, 6, 8 = B calls A.
When you need addresses and telephone numbers, use your own.

1.
> B is a secretary at Union Bank.
> You want to talk to B's boss, Ms.Lee.
> When B answers the phone, say:
>   This is _____ from _____ .
>   (name)   (company)
>   Is Ms. Lee in?

2.
> You work for a company called United Technology.
> Begin by saying:
>   Good _____ . United Technology.
>   (morning)
> Answer B's question.

3.
> B is a travel agent.
> You want to go to Rio de Janerio, Brazil.
> When B answers, say:
>   I'm calling about flights to Rio de Janerio. What time do they leave?
> Find out what time flights are.
> Decide which one you want.

4.
> You are a secretary at Century Trading.
> Your boss, Mr. Sato, is not at the office today.
> Begin by saying:
>   Century Trading. May I help you?
> Ask if B wants
> ■ to call Mr. Sato tomorrow?
> OR
> ■ Mr. Sato to call him/her back?
> Be sure to find out B's phone number:
>   _____-_____

5.
> B works for a company called Intertech.
> You need to send a letter to B.
> Find out the address.
> When B answers, say:
>   This is _____ from _____ .
>   (name)   (company)
>   Could you tell me Intertech's address?

6.
> You work for Universal, Inc.
> Begin by saying:
>   Universal, Incorporated.
>   May I help you?
> Listen to B. Answer.
> Use your own schedule.

7.
> B works for Eastern Printing Co.
> You want to set the time for a meeting next week.
> Find a time when you both are free.
> When B answers, say:
>   Hello. This is _____ from _____ .
>   (name)   (company)
>   I was wondering if we could set up a time to meet next week.

8.
> You are a travel agent.
> Begin by saying:
>   Good _____ . Horizon Travel.
>   (afternoon)
> Answer B's questions.

Time	Flight	Airline
To Kuala Lumpur (KUL)		
1730	MH 83	Malaysia Airlines
To Seoul (SEL)		
1000	KE 633	Korean Air
1240	OZ 131	Asiana
To Singapore (SIN)		
0920	SQ 989	Singapore Airlines
1405	UL 459	Airlanka

┌ ─ ─ *Keep going!* ─ ─ ➤

2 Think of three more messages.
Call B. Leave the messages.
Write B's message.

Writing Right ✍

While you were out...

1 Put the words in the sentences in order. Write the sentences in a memo to your manager, Ms. Tanaka.

1. the ~~Ms. Watts~~ group called tour about
2. our received yesterday fax she
3. flights more she about information the needs
4. could she her asked call if return you
5. time like she up meet to would a set to you
6. is number her 379-2845 phone

Telephone message

TO: _____

FROM: _____
(your name)

DATE: _____
(today)

SUBJECT: *Call from Marie Watts,*
Sunshine Beach Hotel

Ms. Watts _____

_____

_____

_____

2 Choose two of the conversations from the pair work (page 62 and page 107). Write telephone messages.

Numbers 1.2.3.

1 📻 Listen. Write the telephone numbers you hear. Check by saying the numbers.

2 📻 Listen. You will hear the numbers in sentences. Write only the numbers. Check by saying them.

3 👥 Student A, use activity file 14 (page 85). Student B, use activity file 33 (page 90).

15 Complaints

Get ready!

1 👥 Work in pairs. Imagine that you have just taken a business trip. Everything went wrong. Imagine the problems. Write them.

- Airplane: *It was overbooked.* _____
- Hotel: _____
- Weather: _____
- ▪ _____

- Meeting: _____
- Restaurant: _____
- ▪ _____
- ▪ _____

2 Join another pair. Tell your story. Listen to theirs.

I had a terrible trip. First, my plane was overbooked. I had to take a later flight. Then …

Conversation 💬

There's a problem …

1 📻 Listen.

I have a complaint about   the problem
I'm not satisfied with   your complaint

there's no hot water   We'll take care of it
the air-conditioning doesn't work   We'll fix it

another thing   talk to the manager
another problem   see what I can do

Pronunciation focus

2 📻 Listen again. Say the sentences. Match the stress and rhythm.

3 👥 Practice the conversation with a partner.
Then close your book. Have a conversation like this one.

Listening 📼

What a trip!

1 📼 **Listen. A customer is complaining. Which things were problems? Circle them.**

What was wrong?

1.

The waiter

2.

The weather

3.

bus/bus driver

4.

wake-up call

5.

ticket voucher

What was wrong?

6.

hotel room

7.

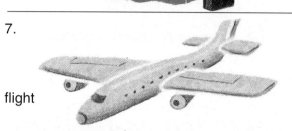

flight

8.

tour guide

It's Culture

Complaining

Ways to complain vary. In English-speaking countries, complaints can be very direct. Remember:

■ Be polite.

■ The person wants action. Say what you'll do and when.

■ If you can't help, say so.

■ If the customer isn't satisfied, call your manager.

How do people complain in your country?

2 📼 **Listen again. What was wrong? Write the complaint. Use some of these words:**

late rude uncomfortable wrong
inexperienced terrible overbooked fast

Group Work

I'll take care of it.

1 First work in pairs. What complaints do people make in these places? Write one more for each.

Hotels

■ My room hasn't been cleaned.

■ The air-conditioner doesn't work.

■ The TV in the next room is too loud.

■ There aren't any towels in the bathroom.

■ _____

Offices, travel agencies and restaurants

■ I ordered something but it hasn't arrived.

■ I've been waiting for 45 minutes!

■ You gave me the wrong tickets.

■ There's a mistake on my bill.

■ _____

2 Student A, choose a problem from exercise 1. Say your complaint:

I'm afraid...

Excuse me...

Student B, choose a response from the box below. Say it. Take turns.

	I'll ask them to turn it down.
I'm very sorry.	I'll check on it.
I'm sorry, sir/ma'am.	I'll have it fixed right now.
	I'll have someone do it right away.
I apologize.	I'll help you right now.
	Let me change them for you.

3 Now, cut out activity file 74 (page 111). Think of three complaints. Write them in the blue boxes. Write responses in the yellow boxes.

4 Cut out the squares. Give them to your teacher. Your teacher will mix all complaints and responses (separately). You will get one of each.

Complaint:

Excuse me.
my food hasn't
come.

Response:

I'm very sorry. I'll...
check on it
right now.

5 Work with the whole class. Say your complaint. When someone's "response" matches, you collect the square.

Listen to people's complaints. If your response matches, say it.

Give the person that square. When your response doesn't match, say:

Just a minute, sir/ma'am.

I'll get the manager.

When you get a match or give away your square, get a new one from the teacher. The person with the most matches is the winner.

Writing Right ✍

Requesting action

When you have a complaint, you need to request action.

1 Read this letter. Circle the part that explains the problem.
Put a check (✔) next to the action requested.
Underline the friendly but direct ending.

Intertech
S O F T W A R E
249 Ocean Street
Seattle
Washington 98239
U.S.A.

Phone: (206) 555-2378
Fax: (206) 555-3894

November 25, (year)

Mr. Tony Kaku
Modern Productions
23490 59th Street
San Francisco, CA 94608

Dear Mr. Kaku:

Our records show that Modern Productions owes $795.00 for the purchase of the **Astrowrite** software program. Payment was due September 21. We have not yet received payment. It is now two months overdue.

Please make this payment immediately.

We look forward to your prompt response and to doing business with you in the future.

Sincerely,

Sean Suzuki

Sean Suzuki
Clerk
Accounting Dept.

2 When you receive a complaint letter, your answer follows this form:

1. *Acknowledge the letter:* Thank you for your letter of (date)
2. *Apologize:* We apologize for being late with the payment.
3. *Give a reason:* The invoice was misplaced.
4. *Say the action you are taking:* Payment will be made today.
5. *Apologize again:* Again, we are sorry for this error.
6. *End politely and positively:* We look forward to working with you in the future.

Write a letter from Mr. Kaku to Mr. Suzuki.

Numbers 1.2.3.

1 📼 Listen. Write the numbers you hear. Check by saying the numbers.

2 📼 Listen. You will hear the numbers in sentences. Write only the numbers. Check by saying them.

3 👥 Student A, use activity file 15 (page 85).
Student B, use activity file 34 (page 90).

16 Advice

— — — — — — Get ready! — — — — — —

1 👥 Work in pairs. Student A, use activity file 53 (page 101).
Student B, use activity file 60 (page 103). Listen to your partner's problem.
What do you think your partner should do? Give your advice.
Read your problem. Listen to your partner's advice. Choose a response:

- ■ That's a good idea.
- ■ I'm not sure.
- ■ Well, maybe...

Conversation 💬

That's a good idea.

1 📻 Listen.

| do | Why not take |
| try | Why don't you take |

| an interesting | A 3-hour |
| a great | An all-day |

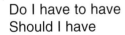

| Do I have to have | need to |
| Should I have | have to |

| Please do that. | You should take |
| All right. | I'd suggest |

Pronunciation focus

2 📻 Listen again. Say the sentences. Match the stress and rhythm.

3 👥 Practice the conversation with a partner.
Then close your book. Have a conversation like this one.

Listening 🔊

What should I do?

1 🔊 **People are giving advice. Listen. What are they talking about?**
Number the pictures 1–5. There is one extra picture.

❑ How should I get to the airport?

❑ What kind of bank account?

❑ Which tour?

❑ I'm too busy at work.

❑ My job is boring.

❑ I'm nervous using English.

2 🔊 **Listen again. How do they give advice? Check (✔) your answers.**

1. ❑ Have you tried talking to the boss?
   ❑ How about talking to your boss?

2. ❑ Why don't you go to Brazil?
   ❑ If I were you, I'd go to Brazil.

3. ❑ If I were you, I'd take an English class.
   ❑ Have you tried taking an English class?

4. ❑ How about a Check Plus account?
   ❑ Have you tried a Check Plus account?

5. ❑ You should take the airport bus.
   ❑ Why don't you take the airport bus?

Group Work 👥👥

I think you should...

1 Cut out activity file 70 (page 108). Fold it so it looks like this.

Problem:
I need to learn more English words.

Advice #1: I think you should...

Advice #2: Why don't you...

Advice #3: Have you tried... ·

Advice #4: How about...

Advice #5: If I were you, I'd...

What problems do people have at work or school? Write at least three problems.

_____

_____

_____

■ Choose one problem. Write it in the top section of your folded paper.

■ Work in groups of six. Sit in a circle. Give your paper to the person to your left. Take the paper from the person on your right.

■ Read the problem. What should your partner do? Write your advice under the problem.

■ Fold the paper so no one can see your advice. Pass it to the person on your left. Take the new one from the person on your right. Read the new problem.

■ Do NOT look at anyone else's advice! Write your advice for the problem. Continue. Write advice for each problem.

■ When you get your paper back, read the problem to the group. Read all the advice. As a group, decide which advice is best. Circle it. Is there any advice you can't follow? Why?

Problem:
I need to learn more English words.

Advice #1: I think you should... *buy some U.S. magazines and newspapers.*

Advice #2: Why don't you...

Advice #3: Have you tried...

Advice #4: How about...

Advice #5: If I were you, I'd...

┌ - - Keep going! - - - - ➤

2 👥👥 **Work in pairs. Choose one of these topics:**

Advice for people starting a new job.
Advice for people looking for a job.
Ways to take care of problems at work.

Talk about your topic for exactly two minutes.

■ Try to speak the entire time. Your partner will listen and tell you when two minutes is over. Partner, at the end, ask at least two questions. Then the partner speaks for two minutes.

■ When you finish, change partners. Try to give the same "mini-speech" in 90 seconds.

■ Finally, change partners again. Can you give the "mini-speech" in 75 seconds?

Writing Right ✍

I'd suggest...

1 Read Mr. Miller's notes.

> Phone call from:
> Tom Jarret
> Student Group Tour,
> 25 people
> July 14 - Aug 10
> Requests information and
> suggestions

> Send: Information and brochures
> Suggestions:
> Southwestern or High Country Tour
> Look over info and brochures;
> call again
> busy season; decide quickly;
> make reservations

2 Complete Mr. Miller's letter. Use his notes and these words:

I think you should   reasonable   tour   hearing   ~~phone call~~

I'd suggest   questions   happy   excellent

PACIFIC TOURS

17 Pan Pacific Place   Phone: (604) 931-0707
Vancouver, B.C. V5G 3L1   Fax: (604) 931-0708

May 3, (year)

Mr. Tom Jarret
3588 Royal Avenue
West Vancouver, B.C. V7W 2B6

Dear Mr. Jarret:

Thank you for your _phone call_ yesterday about your _____ _____ tour for _____ people.

I am sending some _____ and _____ about several different _____. _____ _____ either the Southwestern or _____ _____ tour. They are both _____ tours and the prices are very _____.

Please _____ _____ the enclosed information and brochures and then _____. I'd be _____ to answer any _____ .

Finally, since your trip is during the _____ season, _____ _____ _____ _____ try to _____ quickly and make your _____.

I'm looking forward to _____ from you soon.

Sincerely,

Frank Miller

Frank Miller
Sales Agent

Numbers 1.2.3.

1 🔊 Listen. Write the numbers you hear. Check by saying the numbers.

2 🔊 Listen. You will hear the numbers in sentences. Write only the numbers. Check by saying them.

3 👥 Student A, use activity file 16 (page 85). Student B, use activity file 35 (page 90).

17 Asking permission

- Get ready! -

1 👥 You use these words to:
- give permission (It's OK to do it.)
- show obligation (You must do it.)
- give advice (It's a good idea to do it.)

~~must~~ can should have to need to

Work with a partner. Write the words on the chart.

Now, write the negative for each word (can → can't).

permission		obligation		advice	
_____	_____	*must*	_____	_____	_____
		_____	_____		
		_____	_____		

2 Think about rules at work or school. Say one rule for each of the words.

Conversation 💬

Can I get...

1 📻 Listen.

Excuse me. You have to put your bag under your seat.

Oh, right.

A

need to
should

sorry
OK

You need to fasten your seatbelt.

Can I get a magazine first?

C

have to
should

use the washroom
get a newspaper

I'm sorry but you can't smoke in the plane.

Oh, sorry. I forgot.

B

use a cellular phone
have a radio

pardon me
I'm sorry

Please hurry. You have to be in your seat before we take off.

I'll be right back.

D

must
need to

only be a minute
hurry

Pronunciation focus

2 📻 Listen again. Say the sentences. Match the stress and rhythm.

3 👥 Practice the conversation with a partner.
Then close your book. Have a conversation like this one.

Listening 🔊
Different cultures, different rules

1 🔊 Listen. Number the pictures 1–9.

❑ yes ❑ no

❑ yes ❑ no

❑ yes ❑ no

❑ yes ❑ no

❑ yes ❑ no

❑ yes ❑ no

❑ yes ❑ no

❑ yes ❑ no

❑ yes ❑ no

2 🔊 Listen again. Write at least one more piece of information about each rule. Are the rules the same in your country? Check (✔) yes or no.

It's Culture

Culture "rules"

These are general hints about culture. Some people may act differently.

▪ If you aren't sure what to do, ask!

▪ If you don't understand, ask! People will like your interest. That's good for business.

What customs in your country are hard for foreigners to understand?

Group Work 👥👥

What do you have to do?

1 Think about a job. It can be: the job you have; a job you will have someday; a job you would like to have. Play the game in groups of three.

■ You each need something small (a coin, eraser, etc.) to mark your place.
■ Roll a die 🎲 or use the "How many spaces" box (activity file 68 on page 106). Move that many spaces.
■ Answer the question. Say at least three sentences.
■ Take turns.

START

- - - *Keep going!* - - - - - ➔

2 Divide a piece of paper into three parts:
■ Rules I like.
■ Rules I don't like.
■ Rules I don't like but they are good rules.
Write one rule in each part.

3 Stand up. Find a partner. Say one of your rules. Partner, what do you think of that rule? Write it in the correct part of your paper.

4 Change partners. Continue until you've written at least eight rules.

Writing Right ✎

What are the rules?

1 Look at the picture. What do you think people shouldn't be doing? Circle your guesses.

2 Now, read the office rules. Were you right? Cross out (✗) the things that are against the rules.

Intertech
**OFFICE
POLICY**

◆ **Work begins at 9:00. You have to be on time.**

◆ **Do not smoke in the office. Smoking is allowed only in the smokers' lounge.**

◆ **You must not make personal phone calls during work hours.**

◆ **You should not have food and drinks near the computers.**

◆ **Men have to wear neckties.**

3 What rules do you have to follow at work or school? Write at least five. Use some of these words:

should   shouldn't   have to   don't have to
must   must not   need to   can   can't   don't

Numbers 1.2.3.

1 📼 Listen. Write the numbers you hear. Check by saying the numbers.

2 📼 Listen. You will hear the numbers in sentences. Write only the numbers. Check by saying them.

3 👥 Student A, use activity file 17 (page 86). Student B, use activity file 36 (page 91).

18 Future plans

- - - - - - - - - - - - *Get ready!* - - - - - - - - - - - -

1 Imagine that you are going on a tour. Where will you go? When?
Where will you stay? Circle one of each:

Places: India   China   Canada

Months: December   May   August

Hotels: Plaza   Green   Sun Inn
       (expensive) (average) (cheap)

2 Find other students who chose the same place, month and hotel
as you. Ask the questions. Find the members of your tour.

Where are you going? When are you going there? Where are you going to stay?

Conversation

Someday...

1 Listen.

manager   joking
president   kidding

do a great job
do my best

time off   I'd like that.
responsibility   That sounds good.

late   started
forever   going

Pronunciation focus

2 Listen again. Say the sentences. Match the stress and rhythm.

3 Practice the conversation with a partner.
Then close your book. Have a conversation like this one.

Listening 🔊

What and when?

1 🔊 **Listen. What are these people planning to do? Write the letters (A–G) in the squares. There is one extra action.**

When? Write it. _____

A.
stop by the bank

B.
call

C.
send a fax

D.
type the letters

E.
make a hotel reservation

F.
stay at a hotel

G.
start a new job

1.
Cathy

What? C

When?
this afternoon

2.
Rick

What?

When?

3.
Maria

What?

When?

4.
Larry
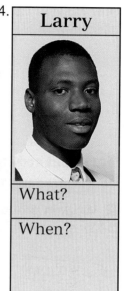
What?

When?

5.
Erika
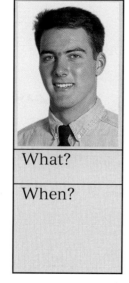
What?

When?

6.
Kent

What?

When?

Remember!

■ Use **be + going to + verb** for things you know will happen:
I'm *going to* meet her tomorrow.
You can also use **be + verb + ing**:
I'm *meeting* her tomorrow.

■ Use **will + verb** if you are saying what you think or hope will happen:
I'll be a manager someday.

■ Also use **will + verb** at the time you decide or when you promise to do something:
BOSS: Have you sent the fax yet?
YOU: I'll send it right now.

2 🔊 **Listen again. Which words do the people use? Check (✔) the boxes.**

1. ☑ going to
   ☐ will
   ☐ sending

2. ☐ going to
   ☐ will
   ☐ typing

3. ☐ going to
   ☐ will
   ☐ starting

4. ☐ going to
   ☐ will
   ☐ calling

5. ☐ going to
   ☐ will
   ☐ stopping

6. ☐ going to
   ☐ will
   ☐ staying

Group Work 👥👥

Your career

Think about your career.
What are your goals?
What are your dreams?
What are you going to do in
the future?
How will your career change?

1 Cut out activity file 73 (page 111). Cut apart the squares.
Fill in each square so it is true about you or your plans.

2 Work in groups of five.
■ Mix everyone's squares together.

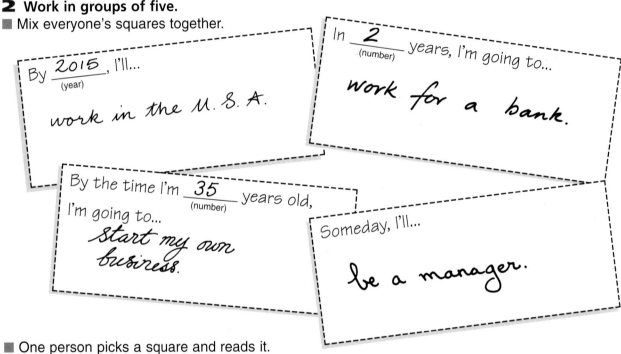

By _2015_ , I'll...
(year)

work in the U.S.A.

In __2__ years, I'm going to...
(number)

work for a bank.

By the time I'm __35__ years old,
(number)
I'm going to...
start my own
business.

Someday, I'll...

be a manager.

■ One person picks a square and reads it.
■ Who do you think wrote it? Say the name:

In two years, Alberto is going to work for a bank.
Someday, Mari will be a manager.

■ If you are correct, you get one point.
If you are wrong, anyone else can guess.
■ The person who guesses correctly picks the next sentence.

╔ − − *Keep going!* − − − − ➤

3 Keep working in your group of five. Imagine that your group is
going to open a new company office. What will you need to do?
Each person adds ideas. Start like this:

First we're going to decide where to open the office.
After we decide where to open the office, we're going to...

Keep the story going as long as possible.

Writing Right ✎
Making plans

1 Complete the memo. Use these future forms:

going to
are going to give
are going to have
is going to meet

ing
are coming
are bringing
are leaving
is taking

will
will check in
will be time
will finish
will probably be busy

MEMO

TO: Rita Park
FROM: Don Barnes
DATE: Oct. 10, (year)
SUB: Sales Meeting in Seattle

We ___*are leaving*___ from the office by car on Thursday, October 12th, at 9:00.
    The roads _____ . If we arrive before 11 a.m., we _____ at the hotel first. Ms. Romero _____ us at the Head Office at noon. We _____ a working lunch in the office. Ms. Romero _____ care of everything. The meeting begins at 2:00, so I think there _____ to relax after lunch.
    The new sales reps. _____ to the meeting, so we _____ the new brochures. We _____ them out in the afternoon.
    I hope the meeting _____ by 6:00.

---

2 Write another travel plan. For example, a staff party, a sightseeing trip or a class picnic. Include these things:
▨ Where, when, how people are going.
▨ What you will do there.
▨ What people should bring.

Numbers 1.2.3.

1 🔲 Listen. Write the numbers. What do you think they mean? Number the boxes.

❏ credit card number
❏ video club card
❏ government identification number (U.S.: social security number)

❏ telephone number
❏ student ID (identification) number
❏ postal code (U.S.: Zip Code)

2 🔲 Listen. Were you right?

3 👥 Student A, use activity file 18 (page 86). Student B, use activity file 37 (page 91).

Review, UNITS 10-18

1 👥 **Work with a partner. This is a speaking contest. You will see how long you can speak in English. Your turn is over when you:**
- ■ **stop for five seconds.**
- ■ **say a word that is not English.**

Partner, listen. Time the speaker. When the speaker finishes, you must ask at least three questions. Then change parts.

Choose one topic:
- ■ **Your job in five years.**
- ■ **The best places to visit in your country.**
- ■ **The best ways for you to learn English.**

Find the mistakes

2 👥 **Work with a partner. Look at these sentences. Each sentence has a mistake. Find the mistakes. Correct them.**

3 📼 **Now listen. Are you right? If you are correct, check (✔) OK. If your answer is wrong, fix it. Then look at the page in parentheses. Find a correct example.**

1. *I'd*
   ~~I~~ like a brochure, please.   (page 48)
2. Turn left to the next corner and go straight.   ☐ OK   (page 45)
3. I'm sorry but can't you smoke here.   ☐ OK   (page 72)
4. The weather's much more better in January.   ☐ OK   (page 52)
5. We're have a meeting in 10 minutes.   ☐ OK   (page 56)
6. Could you tell to her to call me back, please?   ☐ OK   (page 60)
7. I'll take care right away of it.   ☐ OK   (page 64)
8. If I was you, I'd go on the bus tour.   ☐ OK   (page 68)
9. You should need to fasten your seat belt.   ☐ OK   (page 72)
10. Where you are going to meet him?   ☐ OK   (page 76)

There are some other ways to correct the sentences. If you think your answer is right, ask your teacher.

Talking tasks

4 👥 **Work with a partner.**
Student A, look at the talking task cards in activity file 67 (page 106).
Student B, look at the talking task cards in activity file 63 (page 104).

OFFICE FILE

a fluency game (2)

You will review the English you're learned so far.

■ Work in groups of three or four.

■ Put a space marker on "START."

■ Roll a die 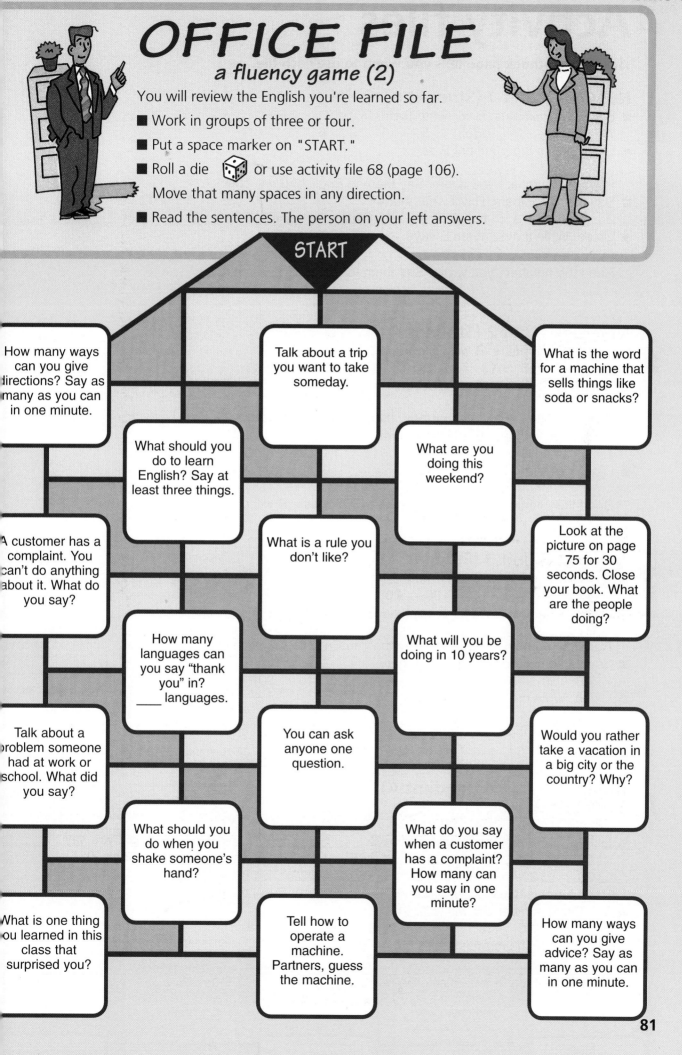 or use activity file 68 (page 106).
Move that many spaces in any direction.

■ Read the sentences. The person on your left answers.

START

How many ways can you give directions? Say as many as you can in one minute.

Talk about a trip you want to take someday.

What is the word for a machine that sells things like soda or snacks?

What should you do to learn English? Say at least three things.

What are you doing this weekend?

A customer has a complaint. You can't do anything about it. What do you say?

What is a rule you don't like?

Look at the picture on page 75 for 30 seconds. Close your book. What are the people doing?

How many languages can you say "thank you" in? ____ languages.

What will you be doing in 10 years?

Talk about a problem someone had at work or school. What did you say?

You can ask anyone one question.

Would you rather take a vacation in a big city or the country? Why?

What should you do when you shake someone's hand?

What do you say when a customer has a complaint? How many can you say in one minute?

What is one thing you learned in this class that surprised you?

Tell how to operate a machine. Partners, guess the machine.

How many ways can you give advice? Say as many as you can in one minute.

Activity files

The main textbook page tells you when to use each file.

1 Numbers - Unit 1 (Student A)
- Say these numbers. B will write them.
  7 4 9 3 0 (oh) 5 10 2 6 1 8
- Listen. Write the numbers B says.

  _____

  Read the numbers you wrote. Say them in English. B will check.
- Say these numbers. B will write them.
  2 3 6 9 1 8 4 7 10 5 0 (oh)
- Listen. Write the numbers B says.

  _____

  Read the numbers you wrote. Say them in English. B will check.

2 Numbers - Unit 2 (Student A)
- Say these numbers. B will write them.
  12 16 18 13 17 10 19 14 11 15
- Listen. Write the numbers B says.

  _____

  Read the numbers you wrote. Say them in English. B will check.
- Say these numbers. B will write them.
  13 17 14 11 19 18 15 12 10 16
- Listen. Write the numbers B says.

  _____

  Read the numbers you wrote. Say them in English. B will check.

3 Numbers - Unit 3 (Student A)
- Say these numbers. B will write them.
  40 10 60 30 90 20 100 70 50 80
- Listen. Write the numbers B says.

  _____

  Read the numbers you wrote. Say them in English. B will check.
- Say these numbers. B will write them.
  50 20 100 70 30 60 90 10 80 40
- Listen. Write the numbers B says.

  _____

  Read the numbers you wrote. Say them in English. B will check.

4 Numbers - Unit 4 (Student A)
- Say these numbers.
  12 13 40 15 60 70 18 90
- Listen. Check (✔) the numbers B says.

  ❑ 12 ❑ 13 ❑ 14 ❑ 15 ❑ 16 ❑ 17 ❑ 18 ❑ 19
  ❑ 20 ❑ 30 ❑ 40 ❑ 50 ❑ 60 ❑ 70 ❑ 80 ❑ 90

  Read the numbers you wrote. Say them in English. B will check.
- Say these numbers. B will write them.
  14 70 20 16 50 17 30 80 19 40
- Listen. Write the numbers B says.

  _____

  Read the numbers you wrote. Say them in English. B will check.

> Did you say **13 or 30**?

Numbers - Unit 5 (Student A)

■ Say these numbers. B will write them.

57   78   29   86   55   34   93   62   49   21

■ Listen. Write the numbers B says.

Read the numbers you wrote. Say them in English. B will check.

■ Say these numbers. B will write them.

81   52   37   24   76   45   39   98   66   73

■ Listen. Write the numbers B says.

Read the numbers you wrote. Say them in English. B will check.

5

Numbers - Unit 6 (Student A)

■ Say these numbers. B will write them.

839   523   142   770   616   360   408   211   904

■ Listen. Write the numbers B says.

Read the numbers you wrote. Say them in English. B will check.

■ Say these numbers. B will write them.

159   686   364   273   550   415   807   990   705

■ Listen. Write the numbers B says.

Read the numbers you wrote. Say them in English. B will check.

6

Numbers - Unit 7 (Student A)

■ Say these times.

■ Listen. Draw the hands on the clocks.

Say the times. B will check.

■ Say these times. B will write them.

a. two o'clock   b. a quarter after twelve   c. a quarter to five   d. half past eight
e. ten after six   f. twenty to eleven   g. nine oh five   h. seven-fifty

■ Listen. Write the times B says.

a. ___:___   b. ___:___   c. ___:___   d. ___:___
e. ___:___   f. ___:___   g. ___:___   h. ___:___

Say the times. B will check.

7

Numbers - Unit 8 (Student A)

B looks at the time zone chart on page 37. Ask B these questions.
Check B 's answers.

1. It's 7:15 pm in Taipei, Taiwan. What time is it in Bangkok?   (Answer: 6:15 pm)
2. It's 9:30 am in Athens, Greece. What time is it in Vancouver?   (11:30 pm)
3. It's 8:45 am in Sydney. What time is it in Rio de Janeiro?   (7:45 pm)
4. It's 4:00 pm in New York. What time is it in Taipei?   (5:00 am)
5. It's 1:30 pm in London. What time is it where you live?   (Find the answer)

Now you look at the time zone chart on page 37. Answer B 's questions.

8

Numbers - Unit 9 (Student A)

9

- Say these numbers. B will write them.

  2,045   3,611   7,777   6,959   9,850   1,557   4,402   8,320

- Listen. Write the numbers B says.

Read the numbers you wrote. Say them in English. B will check.

- Say these numbers. B will write them.

  4,020   3,235   1,368   7,195   8,715   2,119   5,522   9,910

- Listen. Write the numbers B says.

Read the numbers you wrote. Say them in English. B will check.

Numbers - Unit 10 (Student A)

10

- Say these numbers. B will write them.

  ninth   seventy-sixth   forty-second   twenty-eighth
  sixteenth   thirty-first   eighteenth   fifty-fifth

- Listen. Write the numbers B says.

Read the numbers you wrote. Say them in English. B will check.

- Say these numbers. B will write them.

  fifteenth   thirtieth   twelfth   forty-seventh
  twenty-first   eighty-third   tenth   twenty-fourth

- Listen. Write the numbers B says.

Read the numbers you wrote. Say them in English. B will check.

Numbers - Unit 11 (Student A)

11

- Say these numbers. B will write them.

  8.5   3.15   1.22   279.41   14.80   37.77   67.9   0.28

- Listen. Write the numbers B says.

HINT

. = point

Read the numbers you wrote. Say them in English. B will check.

- Say these numbers. B will write them.

  8.3   60.54   416.99   28.35   7.8   988.31   286.7   3.09

- Listen. Write the numbers B says.

Read the numbers you wrote. Say them in English. B will check.

Numbers - Unit 12 (Student A)

12

- Say these sentences. B will write the amounts.

  Seven hundred and twenty-four dollars and ninety-eight cents.   ($724.98)
  Sixty-nine eighty-five.   ($69.85)
  Three-fifty.   ($3.50)

- Check. Then listen. Write the amounts B says.

  $___.___ $___.___ $___.___

- Say these numbers. B will write them.

  $42.19 $802.65 $185.57 $435.18 $5.25
  $758.40 $231.14 $12.50 $1368.45 $948.00

- Listen. Write the amounts B says.

Read the numbers you wrote. Say them in English. B will check.

Numbers - Unit 13 (Student A)

■ Say these letters and numbers. B will write them.

ON512-79	MW53490	CX179	T86451
U37718L	DM650-30	PB11095	OZ952

■ Listen. Write the letters and numbers B says.

Read the letters and numbers you wrote. Say them in English. B will check.

■ Say these letters and numbers. B will write them.

S786 31Z	TW 281	CL 435-44	IR 66421
HC 570-49	K89936	SQ 195	JP11 D28

■ Listen. Write the letters and numbers B says.

Read the letters and numbers you wrote. Say them in English. B will check.

In U.S. English, z = zee /ziː/. In most other English-speaking countries, z = zed /zɛd/.

– = a short pause
0 = oh

13

Numbers - Unit 14 (Student A)

■ Say these telephone numbers. B will write them.

274-5810	955-0113	450-2101	735-4266
394-9360	830-2157	583-2478	681-6464

■ Listen. Write the telephone numbers B says.

Read the numbers you wrote. Say them in English. B will check.

■ Say these telephone numbers. B will write them.

888-3691	347-3271	805-6444	281-8905
679-8325	471-7471	262-8512	703-4638

■ Listen. Write the telephone numbers B says.

Read the numbers you wrote. Say them in English. B will check.

14

Numbers - Unit 15 (Student A)

■ Say these numbers. B will write them.

21,916	50,119	89,333	98,181	67,522	39,737	54,750

■ Listen. Write the numbers B says.

Read the numbers you wrote. Say them in English. B will check.

■ Say these numbers. B will write them.

99,934	68,440	36,253	23,586	47,368	75,627	80,584

■ Listen. Write the numbers B says.

Read the numbers you wrote. Say them in English. B will check.

15

Numbers - Unit 16 (Student A)

■ Say these numbers. B will write them.

729,102	232,088	124,600	293,761	978,998	604,543

■ Listen. Write the numbers B says.

Read the numbers you wrote. Say them in English. B will check.

■ Say these numbers. B will write them.

615,020	148,304	457,159	734,111	501,917	397,374

■ Listen. Write the numbers B says.

Read the numbers you wrote. Say them in English. B will check.

16

17 Numbers - Unit 17 (Student A)

- Say these numbers. B will write them.

95,266,202	6,743,884	37,328,006	8,118,167
5,292,453	2,050,721	78,795,899	49,527,345

- Listen. Write the numbers B says.

Read the numbers you wrote. Say them in English. B will check.

- Say these numbers. B will write them.

17,555,620	76,819,413	4,238,955	15,351,002
28,439,546	5,938,791	83,140,068	3,689,474

- Listen. Write the numbers B says.

Read the numbers you wrote. Say them in English. B will check.

18 Numbers - Unit 18 (Student A)

Think of numbers in your life. You can use addresses, phone numbers, dates, club membership numbers, etc.

- Say a number. B will guess:
  Is (number) your (video club membership number)?
- Guess B's numbers. Continue.

19 Review, Units 1-9 (Student A)

Talking tasks. Read each card. Do the task with B.

1
- You are starting a new job. B works in the office. How do you introduce yourself? Say at least three sentences. Answer B's questions.
- Listen to B. Ask at least three questions about what B says.

2
- You work at a hotel. B is checking in. Ask questions to fill out a registration form.
- You are opening a bank account. B works at the bank. Answer B's questions.

3
- You work for Century Trading. B will call you. B will suggest a time to meet. You are busy that day. Suggest a different day and time.

4
- You work at a job center. B wants a job. Ask about things B can do, likes to do and is good at.
  Can you...?
  Do you like to...?
  Are you good at...?
  What job do you suggest?
- Now change. You want a job. Answer B's questions.

5
- Find three things you and B both did last weekend.
- Then find three things B did that you didn't do.

6
- Tell B how to draw this picture.

Use these words:

○ circle   —— line
□ square   ☆ star
△ triangle

- Draw the picture B describes.

Numbers - Unit 1 (Student B)

■ Listen. Write the numbers A says.

_____

Read the numbers you wrote. Say them in English. A will check.
■ Say these numbers. A will write them.
  6   9   1   7   5   10   2   4   3   0 (oh)   8
■ Listen. Write the numbers A says.

_____

Read the numbers you wrote. Say them in English. A will check.
■ Say these numbers. A will write them.
  8   4   7   3   6   9   1   0 (oh)   5   2   10

20

Numbers - Unit 2 (Student B)

■ Listen. Write the numbers A says.

_____

Read the numbers you wrote. Say them in English. A will check.
■ Say these numbers. A will write them.
  18   14   11   17   10   15   13   16   12   19
■ Listen. Write the numbers A says.

_____

Read the numbers you wrote. Say them in English. A will check.
■ Say these numbers. A will write them.
  11   15   18   14   13   17   10   19   16   12

21

Numbers - Unit 3 (Student B)

■ Listen. Write the numbers A says.

_____

Read the numbers you wrote. Say them in English. A will check.
■ Say these numbers. A will write them.
  10   50   80   40   70   100   20   60   90   30
■ Listen. Write the numbers A says.

_____

Read the numbers you wrote. Say them in English. A will check.
■ Say these numbers. A will write them.
  80   40   90   10   50   30   70   20   100   60

22

Numbers - Unit 4 (Student B)

■ Listen. Check (✔) the numbers A says.
  ❑ 12   ❑ 13   ❑ 14   ❑ 15   ❑ 16   ❑ 17   ❑ 18   ❑ 19
  ❑ 20   ❑ 30   ❑ 40   ❑ 50   ❑ 60   ❑ 70   ❑ 80   ❑ 90
  Read the numbers you wrote. Say them in English. A will check.
■ Say these numbers.
  20   13   40   50   16   70   18   19
■ Listen. Write the numbers A says.

_____

Read the numbers you wrote. Say them in English. A will check.
■ Say these numbers. A will write them.
  17   80   14   60   19   30   12   16   15   90

Did you say **13** or **30**?

23

24 Numbers - Unit 5 (Student B)

Listen. Write the numbers A says.

_____

Read the numbers you wrote. Say them in English. A will check.
- Say these numbers. A will write them.
    74   33   85   48   64   27   56   41   69   92
- Listen. Write the numbers A says.

_____

Read the numbers you wrote. Say them in English. A will check.
- Say these numbers. A will write them.
    35   67   46   91   59   88   71   22   84   43

25 Numbers - Unit 6 (Student B)

- Listen. Write the numbers A says.

_____

Read the numbers you wrote. Say them in English. A will check.
- Say these numbers. A will write them.
    258   330   611   109   762   440   814   903   517
- Listen. Write the numbers A says.

_____

Read the numbers you wrote. Say them in English. A will check.
- Say these numbers. A will write them.
    974   243   480   308   129   806   635   513   730

26 Numbers - Unit 7 (Student B)

- Listen. Draw the hands on the clocks.

Say the times. A will check.
- Say these times.

- Listen. Write the times A says.
    a. ___:___   b. ___:___   c. ___:___   d. ___:___
    e. ___:___   f. ___:___   g. ___:___   h. ___:___
    Say the times. A will check.
- Say these times. A will write them.
    a. eight o'clock   b. a quarter to ten   c. half past eleven   d. a quarter after nine
    e. twenty after three   f. five to one   g. ten after four   h. ten ten

27 Numbers - Unit 8 (Student B)

First, you look at the time zone chart on page 37. Answer A's questions.
Then A looks at the time zone chart on page 37.
Ask questions. Check A's answers.
1. It's 2:30 pm in New York. What time is it in Rio de Janeiro?   (Answer: 4:30 pm)
2. It's 9:45 am in Vancouver. What time is it in Sydney?   (3:45 pm)
3. It's 3:00 pm in Bangkok. What time is it in Athens?   (10:00 am)
4. It's 1:15 pm in London. What time is it in New York?   (8:15 am)
5. It's 11:30 in New York. What time is it where you live?   (Find the answer)

Numbers - Unit 9 (Student B)

28

- Listen. Write the numbers A says.

Read the numbers you wrote. Say them in English. A will check.
- Say these numbers. A will write them.
  7,460   8,376   4,666   2,045   8,117   3,798   9,169   3,792
- Listen. Write the numbers A says.

Read the numbers you wrote. Say them in English. A will check.
- Say these numbers. A will write them.
  9,009   7,214   8,308   2,584   9,431
  1,811   3,630   4,916   5,346   3,454

Numbers - Unit 10 (Student B)

29

- Listen. Write the numbers A says.

Read the numbers you wrote. Say them in English. A will check.
- Say these numbers. A will write them.
  twenty-fifth   sixth   ninetieth   fourteenth
  sixty-first   thirteenth   eleventh   fifty-third
- Listen. Write the numbers A says.

Read the numbers you wrote. Say them in English. A will check.
- Say these numbers. A will write them.
  twentieth   eighth   seventy-third   twenty-ninth
  eighty-fourth   twelfth   twenty-seventh   second

Numbers - Unit 11 (Student B)

30

- Listen. Write the numbers A says.

Read the numbers you wrote. Say them in English. A will check.
- Say these numbers. A will write them.
  3.4   15.92   287.02   12.99   54.3   339.15   505.6   10.07
- Listen. Write the numbers A says.

HINT
. = point

Read the numbers you wrote. Say them in English. A will check.
- Say these numbers. A will write them.
  673.85   45.10   9.3   38.1   914.2   545.26   0.65   50.15

Numbers - Unit 12 (Student B)

31

- Listen. Write the amounts A says.
  $___.___ $___.___ $___.___
- Check. Then say these sentences. A will write the amounts.
  Sixty-eight dollars and forty-five cents.   ($68.45)
  Three oh five, ninety-eight.   ($305.98)
  Fourteen-fifty.   ($14.50)
- Listen. Write the amounts A says.

- Check. Then say these numbers. A will write them.
  $12.68 $629.60 $874.16 $2.50 $409.23
  $123.60 $7.25 $932.83 $3285.00 $249.95
  Read the numbers you wrote. Say them in English. A will check.

Numbers - Unit 13 (Student B)

32

■ Listen. Write the letters and numbers A says.

Read the letters and numbers you wrote. Say them in English. A will check.
■ Say these letters and numbers. A will write them.
FZ625   W55807G   H7C B44   LC303-55
UI25148   NZ967   VP6 39T   OF617-32
■ Listen. Write the letters and numbers A says.

Read the letters and numbers you wrote. Say them in English. A will check.
■ Say these letters and numbers. A will write them.
SU 96721   RX 504   F70458   RA3 9GZ
PY 500-41   CL 307   BR 41637   MK 981-31

In U.S. English, z = zee /ziː/. In most other English-speaking countries, z = zed /zɛd/.

− = a short pause
0 = oh

Numbers - Unit 14 (Student B)

33

■ Listen. Write the telephone numbers A says.

Read the numbers you wrote. Say them in English. A will check.
■ Say these telephone numbers. A will write them.
963-5424   737-9412   236-4288   718-1101
857-6161   580-0265   329-1422   495-5111
■ Listen. Write the telephone numbers A says.

Read the numbers you wrote. Say them in English. A will check.
■ Say these telephone numbers. A will write them.
742-0923   414-2053   866-4328   213-5566
592-7600   971-7216   332-3248   602-5461

Numbers - Unit 15 (Student B)

34

■ Listen. Write the numbers A says.

Read the numbers you wrote. Say them in English. A will check.
■ Say these numbers. A will write them.
40,702   76,181   28,243   59,308   83,214   32,490   61,800
■ Listen. Write the numbers A says.

Read the numbers you wrote. Say them in English. A will check.
■ Say these numbers. A will write them.
78,979   49,169   17,155   81,857   52,792   20,450   95,326

Numbers - Unit 16 (Student B)

35

■ Listen. Write the numbers A says.

Read the numbers you wrote. Say them in English. A will check.
■ Say these numbers. A will write them.
675,220   981,343   440,006   756,272   161,957   999,343
■ Listen. Write the numbers A says.

Read the numbers you wrote. Say them in English. A will check.
■ Say these numbers. A will write them.
581,014   805,844   282,439   684,407   762,533   324,917

Numbers - Unit 17 (Student B)

- Listen. Write the numbers A says.

36

Read the numbers you wrote. Say them in English. A will check.
- Say these numbers. A will write them.

61,800,440	1,049,198	16,957,600	54,501,727
9,343,856	68,476,095	35,088,105	3,865,413

- Listen. Write the numbers A says.

Read the numbers you wrote. Say them in English. A will check.
- Say these numbers. A will write them.

47,417,612	75,272,555	8,056,932	9,110,704
50,711,330	2,333,247	89,000,886	6,540,679

Numbers - Unit 18 (Student B)

Think of numbers in your life. You can use addresses, phone numbers, dates, club membership numbers, etc.
- Say a number. A will guess:
  Is (number) your (video club membership number?)
- Guess A's numbers. Continue.

37

Review, Units 1-9 (Student B)

Talking tasks. Read each card. Do the task with A.

38

1
- A is starting a new job. You work in the office. Listen to A. Ask at least three questions about what A says.
- Now introduce yourself. Say at least three sentences. Answer A's questions.

2
- A works at a hotel. You are checking in. Answer A's questions.
- You work in a bank. A is opening an account. Ask for A's name, address and telephone number.

3
- A works for Century Trading.
- Call A on the telephone. Make an appointment to meet.

4
- A works at a job center. You want a job. Answer A's questions.
- Now change. You work at the job center. A wants a job. Ask about things A can do, likes to do and is good at.
  Can you...?
  Do you like to...?
  Are you good at...?
  What job do you suggest?

5
- Find three things you and A both did last weekend.
- Then find three things A did that you didn't do.

6
- Draw the picture A describes. Use these shapes:

  ○ circle   —— line
  □ square   ☆ star
  △ triangle

- Tell A how to draw this picture.

Pair Work B

Where are you from?

39

What's	Ms. Reed's Mr. Lee's your		first name?	It's		Maya. Sam. ...
Where	is	she he	from?	She's He's	from	Seattle. Taipei.
	are	you		I'm		......
Where	does	she he	work? go to school?	At	Intertech Software. Union Bank.	
	do	you				
What	does	she he	do?	She's He's	a	secretary. bank teller.
	do	you		I'm		student.

1 Fill in the missing information. Ask A for the information you need.

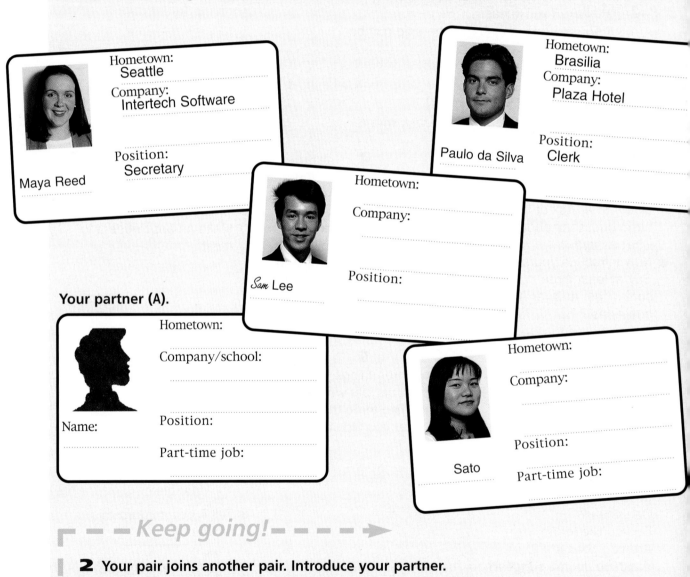

Hometown: Seattle
Company: Intertech Software
Position: Secretary
Maya Reed

Hometown: Brasilia
Company: Plaza Hotel
Position: Clerk
Paulo da Silva

Hometown:
Company:
Position:
Sam Lee

Your partner (A).

Hometown:
Company/school:
Position:
Name:
Part-time job:

Hometown:
Company:
Position:
Sato
Part-time job:

‒ ‒ ‒ *Keep going!* ‒ ‒ ‒ ‒ ➤

2 Your pair joins another pair. Introduce your partner.

This is _____. She's a _____.

Listen to the introductions of the other pair. Ask more questions. Try to learn at least two things about each person.

Pair Work B
Understanding what you hear

1. How do you spell it?	6. I don't know.
2. What does that mean?	7. Pardon?
3. Could you repeat that?	8. Excuse me?
4. How do you say that in English?	9. Did you say 14 or 40?
5. I don't understand.	

1 **Work with A. Which phrases do you use for each problem?**
Write the numbers.
What do you say when:
a. you want someone to say something again? ___*3*___ , ___ or ___
b. you don't know how to write a word? ___
c. you don't know the meaning of a word? ___
d. you don't know how to say a word in English? ___
e. you aren't sure which number you heard? ___
f. you don't know the meaning of a question ___
g. you don't know the answer to a question ___

2 **A will close the book. Ask the questions from exercise 1.**
Use this order: c - b - f - a - g - d - e. A will answer.
What do you say when you don't know the meaning of a word?

Then close your book. A will ask questions. Say the correct phrases.

3 **Follow A's instructions. Draw the picture in the box. When you**
don't understand, ask. Use the phrases in the blue box.

```



```

Now, read the instructions below.
Answer A's questions.
A will draw this picture.

1. Draw two parallel lines.
2. Write the word "parallel" between them.
3. (speak very fast) Write "seventy" to the left of the lines.
4. (speak very softly) Draw a star at the top of the box.

```
        ★
70  ─────────
      parallel
    ─────────
```

- - -*Keep going!*- - - - - ➡

4 **Listen to A. Use the phrases in the blue box.**
When you use one, check it (✔).

5 **Then, think of the job you have or will have someday.**
- ■ Where do you work?
- ■ What do you like about the job?
- ■ What don't you like about the job?
- ■ What things are difficult?

Tell A about the job. Answer A's questions.

Pair Work B 👥
The best job for you

41

1 Fill in the chart. Ask A for the information.

✔ = Yes   ✗ = No   ● = a little   ? = He/she doesn't know.
I don't know.

	Can she ...? Can he...? Can you...?			Does she like...? Does he like ...? Do you like...?		Is she good at...? Is he good at ...? Are you good at...?		
	type	use a computer	speak another language	to meet people	to travel	math	selling things	public speaking
Karen	✔ 75 wpm*	✔	● She can speak a little Portuguese	✗	✗	●		
Carl	___ wpm		✗	✔		✔		?
Sofia	___ wpm	✗	✔ Spanish				✔	✔
Ken	● _35_ wpm		● *Japanese*		✗	✔		✗
Jan	✔ 60 wpm	✔		✔	✔	✔	✔	
A, your partner	___ wpm							

*wpm = words per minute.
Karen can type 75 words in one minute.

2 With A, decide on one job for each person. Write the job next to the name.
tour guide   hotel clerk   bank clerk
travel agent   secretary   salesperson   Other:_____

⌐ ─ ─ Keep going! ─ ─ ─ ─ ➡

**3 Find at least three job skills (typing, using a computer, etc.) you
and A both have. Then find at least three skills A has that you don't.**

Pair Work B 👥

I'd like a room.

1 You are a hotel guest. You are checking into the Plaza Hotel. Ask about the prices. Decide the room you want. Answer A's questions. **Ask these questions:**

■ Is there swimming pool?
■ What time is check out?
■ Where's the business center?
■ How do I get a wake up call?

2 Now you are the clerk at the Lakeview Hotel.
A is a guest. Fill in the form for A.
Answer A's questions.

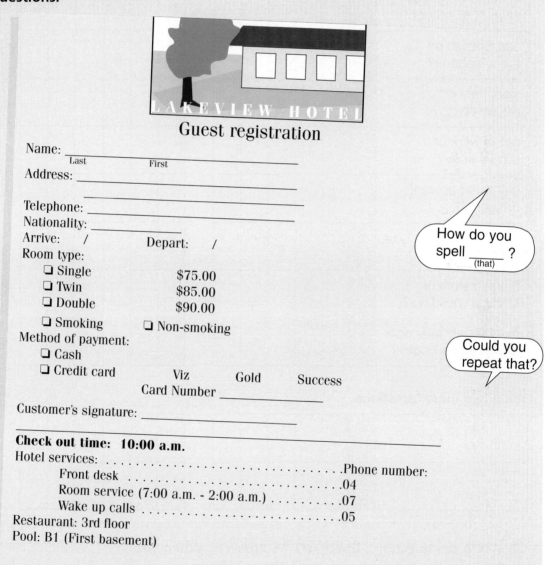

LAKEVIEW HOTEL

Guest registration

Name: _____
     Last   First

Address: _____
_____

Telephone: _____
Nationality: _____
Arrive: /   Depart: /
Room type:
  ❏ Single $75.00
  ❏ Twin $85.00
  ❏ Double $90.00
  ❏ Smoking   ❏ Non-smoking
Method of payment:
  ❏ Cash
  ❏ Credit card   Viz   Gold   Success
             Card Number _____

Customer's signature: _____

Check out time: 10:00 a.m.
Hotel services: . . . .
    Front desk . . . . .Phone number:
    Room service (7:00 a.m. - 2:00 a.m.) 04
    Wake up calls 07
Restaurant: 3rd floor 05
Pool: B1 (First basement)

> How do you spell ___ ?
>   (that)

> Could you repeat that?

- - Keep going! - - - - ➤

3 Close your book. With A, how many things from the form can you remember? What other items are on hotel registration forms in your country? How would you ask for this information? Write one question for each item.

Pair Work B 👥
How often?

43 **1** Read the questions. Check (✔) the answers for yourself.

How often do you...	You always	usually/almost always	often	sometimes	hardly ever/rarely	never	A always	usually/almost always	often	sometimes	hardly ever/rarely	never
become very busy at work or school?												
use English on the telephone?												
sleep late on the weekend?												
get to work or school early?												
get bored at work or school?												
write letters in English?												
have to work or study on holidays?												
meet friends after work or school on Friday?												

Write two more questions.

2 Ask A the questions. Check (✔) A's answers. When you and A have the same answer, circle the question.

How often do you work on weekends?   I ⎰ usually   do.
                                         ⎱ hardly ever

┌ ─ ═Keep going!═ ─ ─ ─ ─ ➡

3 Find at least five things A does more often than you.
Find at least five things you do more often than A.

Pair Work B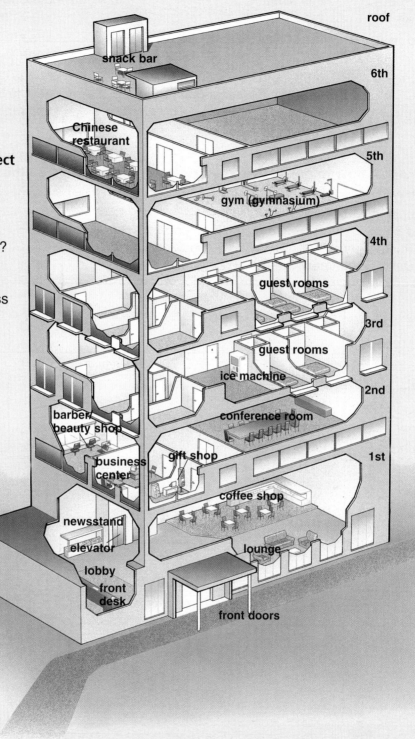
Where can I find it?

1 Look at the hotel. Ask A where these places are:

- the French restaurant
- the swimming pool
- the public telephone
- the parking lot
- the suites
- the nightclub

Write the words in the correct place.

2 Answer A's questions.

EXAMPLE:
Where's the conference room?
It's on the second floor.
It's to the right of the elevator.
The conference room is across from the gift shop.

44

roof

snack bar

6th

Chinese restaurant

5th

gym (gymnasium)

4th

guest rooms

3rd

guest rooms

ice machine

2nd

barber/ beauty shop

conference room

business center

gift shop

1st

coffee shop

tennis courts

newsstand

elevator

lounge

lobby

front desk

front doors

- - - *Keep going!* - - - - ➔

3 Describe the place where you work or your room at home. A, draw a picture of it. When you don't understand something, ask. Was the picture correct?

Pair Work B 👥

Turn right and then...

Go down	this street	to	8th Street.
Take	6th Street		the corner of 6th and Broadway.
Go past	the bookstore.	Go	straight to the second street.
			north to the park.
Turn	right (at the bookstore).	It's	on the corner.
	left (at the second street).		next to the hotel.
			the first building on the right.

1 **Ask A how to get to these places. Write the numbers on the map.**
Answer A's questions. Take turns.

Excuse me. How do I get to ... ?

2. a bank
4. Pacific Airways
6. Day's Department Store

8. a computer store
10. the telephone company
12. the bus station

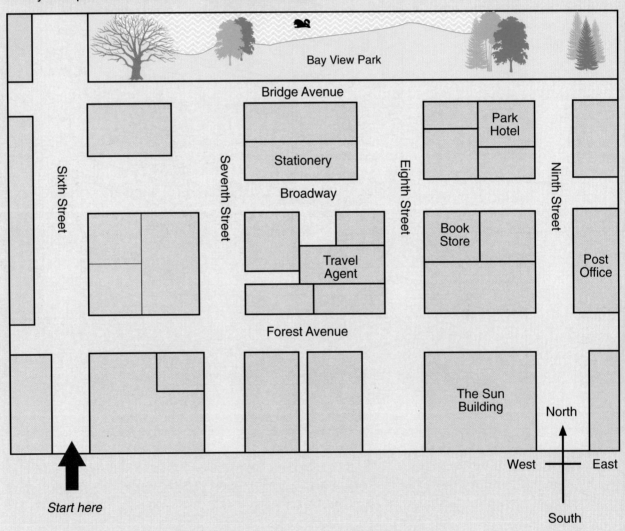

- - - Keep going! - - - - ➤

2 **What are the best places in your area for a tourist to visit?**
Think of at least five places. Tell A. Listen to A's ideas. Together,
decide the six best places. Write directions to each one.

Pair Work B 👥

Find the differences.

1 A's picture is a little different than yours.
What are the people doing? Ask about A's picture. Tell about your picture.
Find the differences. Circle them.

A: What's Ms. Shaw doing?
B: She's waiting in line.
A: In my picture, she's checking in.

A: Is Karen checking in?
B: No, she's waiting in line.

- - - Keep going! - - - - →

2 A, look around the room for one minute. Try to remember what everyone
is doing. Then close your eyes.
B, say what people are doing. Say four sentences. One sentence is wrong.
A, try to find the "mistake." Then change parts. Continue.

Ms. Wade is standing in the back of the room.
Tanya is talking to Roberto.
Ken is asking a question.
Ruth is writing something.

47 Unit 5 – *Get ready!* (Student A)

Read the hints. Your partners will try to guess the words.

Hints:	Words:
1. A room with two beds.	twin (room)
2. A place for swimming.	pool
3. The place guests check in and check out.	front desk (or reception)
4. A place guests can exercise.	gym (health club)
5. They will bring food to guests' rooms	room service

48 Unit 7- *Get ready!* (Student A)

Ask when B does these things. Say what time you do them. Who does them first? Check (✔) your answers.

What time do you...		Who is first?		
		You	B	the same
1. get up?	_____	☐	☐	☐
2. leave for work or school?	_____	☐	☐	☐
3. get home at night?	_____	☐	☐	☐
4. eat dinner?	_____	☐	☐	☐
5. take a shower or bath?	_____	☐	☐	☐

49 Unit 8 – *Get ready!* (Student A)

Read the main verbs to your partners. Listen to their sentences. Make sure they use the correct past tense verbs.

Main verb	Past tense verb	Main verb	Past tense verb	Main verb	Past tense verb
1. stay	(stayed)	4. see	(saw)	7. change	(changed)
2. go	(went)	5. be	(was/were)	8. forget	(forgot)
3. do	(did)	6. talk	(talked)	9. wait	(waited)

50 Unit 11- Group Work (Student A)

Read these instructions to B and C.
Do NOT say the name of the process.

1. a. To start, press the "on" button.
   b. Enter the numbers.
   c. Press "plus", "minus", "times" or "divided by."
   Process: Using a calculator

2. a. First, turn the machine on.
   b. Put in paper.
   c. Finally, begin typing.
   Process: Using an electronic typewriter

3. a. First, put in the money.
   b. Then, press the button for the one you want.
   c. After that, take it out of the machine.
   Process: Using a vending machine

4. a. To begin, write the date at the top.
   b. After that, sign it in front of the teller.
   c. Then, show the teller your passport.
   Process: Cashing a traveler's check

5. a. To begin, turn on the power.
   b. Then, put in the disk.
   c. Finally, open your file and begin.
   Process: Using a computer

6. a. First, give your ticket to the agent.
   b. Then, check in your luggage.
   c. Last, get your boarding pass.
   Process: Checking in at the airport

Unit 12 - Group Work (Travel Agent 1)

Does the hotel have	a swimming pool? restaurants? air-conditioning?	Yes, it does. No, it doesn't.
Where is the hotel located?		It's on the beach.
How far is it from the town center?		It's only a 15 minute walk.
Are meals tours included (in the package)?		Yes, breakfast is included. No, they aren't included.
How much does the tour cost?		Two thousand dollars including air-fare.

1 You are a travel agent. You work for Horizon Travel.
Tell customers about your company's tour to Mystic Island.
You want them to buy your tour.

The Plaza Hotel
first class ★★★★★

- Deluxe, air-conditioned rooms
- Location:
  on quiet, private beach
- Swimming pool, health club
- Free shuttle bus to town center (20 mins.)
- 3 restaurants (Japanese, European and local)
- Bar and Night Club
- Price: $ 3,000 (including air-fare)
- Breakfast, Lunch and Island Tour included

HORIZON TRAVEL

Keep going!
2 Change parts. Travel agents become customers. Customers become agents. Ask the agents about tours to a place in your country. Decide which tour you want to take.

Unit 13 - *Get ready!* (Student A)

Pantomime these actions. Your partners will guess what you are doing.
You are... 1. ...standing in line.
2. ...giving someone directions.
3. ...using a computer.
4. ...reading a funny book.
5. ...checking into a hotel
   They lost your reservation.

Unit 16 - *Get ready!* (Student A)

1. **I'm too busy at work.**
2. (Give B your advice) I think you should...
   EXAMPLES: I think you should find a better job.
   I think you should ask for a raise.
3. **Sometimes I don't really understand what I should do at work.**
4. Why don't you...
5. **I get worried when I have to speak English.**
6. Have you tried ...?
7. **The new person at work is very shy.**
   I'd like to get to know him/her but it is difficult.
8. How about ...?
9. **I can't use the computer very well.**
10. If I were you, I'd...

54 Unit 5 - *Get ready!* (Student B)

Read the hints. Your partners will try to guess the words.

Hints:	Words:
1. A room with one large bed	double (room)
2. A place with computers, fax machines, etc. for guests	business center
3. The time guests must leave the hotel	check out time
4. Guests can get coffee and tea here	coffee shop
5. A place with music and dancing	(night)club

55 Unit 7- *Get ready!* (Student B)

Ask when A does these things. Say what time you do them.
Who does them first? Check (✔) your answers.

		Who is first?		
What time do you...		A	You	the same
1. get up on weekends?	_____	☐	☐	☐
2. eat breakfast?	_____	☐	☐	☐
3. get to work or school?	_____	☐	☐	☐
4. leave work or school?	_____	☐	☐	☐
5. go to bed?	_____	☐	☐	☐

56 Unit 8- *Get ready!* (Student B)

Read the main verbs to your partners. Listen to their sentences.
Make sure they use the correct past tense verbs.

Main verb	Past tense verb	Main verb	Past tense verb	Main verb	Past tense verb
1. finish	(finished)	4. take	(took)	7. cancel	(canceled)
2. fly	(flew)	5. write	(wrote)	8. get	(got)
3. make	(made)	6. leave	(left)	9. reserve	(reserved)

57 Unit 11- Group Work (Student B)

Read these instructions to A and C.
Do NOT say the name of the process.

1. a. First, put in the card.
   b. Listen for the dial tone.
   c. Finally, dial the number.
   Process: Using a phone card

2. a. To start, give the teller some money.
   b. Sign the form.
   c. Last, take the money and receipt.
   Process: Changing money

3. a. To begin, press "start".
   b. Then, type the word you want.
   c. Wait for the translation.
   Process: Using an electronic translator

4. a. First, put the paper into the feeder,
   b. After that, press the "ready" button.
   c. Press the "print" key on the computer.
   Process: Using a computer printer

5. a. First, sign the check-in card.
   b. Then, pay for the first night.
   c. After that, take your room key.
   Process: Checking in to a hotel

6. a. To start, put the cassette in.
   b. Then, set the channel.
   c. Finally, press "record."
   Process: Using a video recorder

Unit 12 - Group Work (Travel Agent 2)

Does the hotel have	a swimming pool? restaurants? air-conditioning?	Yes, it does. No, it doesn't.
Where is the hotel located?		It's on the beach.
How far is it from the town center?		It's only a 15 minute walk.
Are meals tours	included (in the package)?	Yes, breakfast is included. No, they aren't included.
How much does the tour cost?		Two thousand dollars including air-fare.

1 You are a travel agent. You work for Sunshine Travel.
Tell customers about your company's tour to Mystic Island.
You want them to buy your tour.

THE SANDS HOTEL
★★★

☐ Air- conditioned rooms
☐ Location: on the popular
White Sands Beach:
15-minute walk to the town's
exciting nightlife area.
☐ Coffee shop
☐ Breakfast included
☐ Island Tour, available at
$50 extra, per person.
☐ Price: $2,500 (including air-fare)

**Sunshine
Travel Agency**

Keep going!
2 Change parts. Travel agents become customers. Customers become
agents. Ask the agents about tours to a place in your country. Decide
which tour you want to take.

Unit 13 - *Get ready!* (Student B)

Pantomime these actions. Your partners will guess what you are doing.
You are...   1. ...talking on the phone.   4. ...carrying a heavy suitcase.
2. ...looking out the window.   5. ...waiting for a bus. The bus is late.
3. ...dialing the telephone.

.

Unit 16 - *Get ready!* (Student B)

1. (Give A your advice) Why don't you...?
EXAMPLES: Why don't you talk to your boss?
Why don't you find a different job?
2. **I don't make enough money.**
3. Have you tried ...?
4. **I always lose my pens.**
5. How about ...?
6. **Sometimes I get bored at work.**
7. I think you should...
8. **I was late for work (or school) again today.**
9. If I were you, I'd...
10. **Sometimes it is difficult to remember English words.**

61 Unit 5 - *Get ready!* (Student C)

Read the hints. Your partners will try to guess the words.

Hints:	Words:
1. Several connected rooms. It is expensive.	suite
2. A large room for business meetings.	a meeting room (or conference room)
3. A place to get food.	restaurant
4. A phone call at a set time in the morning.	wake-up call
5. A room that is very hot. This is often near the pool or gym.	sauna

62 Unit 8- *Get ready!* (Student C)

Read the main verbs to your partners. Listen to their sentences.
Make sure they use the correct past tense verbs.

Main verb	Past tense verb	Main verb	Past tense verb	Main verb	Past tense verb
1. miss	(missed)	4. say	(said)	7. meet	(met)
2. buy	(bought)	5. arrive	(arrived)	8. spend	(spent)
3. get	(got)	6. call	(called)	9. check in	(checked in)

63 Review, Units 10-18 (Student B)

Talking Tasks. Read each card. Do the task with A.

1

■ Listen to A's directions. Guess the place.

■ Now you think of a well-known place. Don't tell A the place. Give directions from here to the place. A will guess.

2

■ A works for Horizon Travel. You want to talk to Ms. Johnson, the manager. Call A.

■ You work for Union Bank. A will call. Answer A's question. Use information about yourself.

3

You and A are going to another country. What should you do before you go? Think of at least five things.
We should...
We have to...
We need to...

4

■ You are a guest at the Grand Hotel. There are many things wrong with your room. The air conditioner doesn't work. The room hasn't been cleaned. The people in the next room are having a noisy party. A works at the front desk. Call A. Say your complaints and what you want done.

■ You are a travel agent. You sold A a tour. Listen to A. Respond.

5

How many things are you and A doing right now?
We're sitting in class.
We're speaking English.
Think of at least eight more things.

6

■ Find three things you and A are both going to do during the next vacation.

■ Then find three things A is going to do that you aren't.

Unit 11- Group Work (Student C)

Read these instructions to A and B. Do NOT say the name of the process.

64

1.a. To begin, fill out the form.
  b. Then, pay the teller.
  c. Finally, take the draft and statement.
  Process: Getting a bank draft
2.a. First, put in the card.
  b. Then, enter your secret ID number.
  c. After that enter the amount.
  Process: Using a bank card
3.a. To start, fill in the landing card.
  b. Then, hand in the card and your passport.
  c. Last, take your passport and go to Customs.
  Process: Going through passport control

4.a. To start, place the original on the glass.
  b. Then, select the number you want.
  c. Finally, push the "copy" button.
  Process: Using a photocopier
5.a. First, make your recording.
  b. Then, play it back to check.
  c. Finally, set the machine on "Answer mode."
  Process: Using an answering machine
6.a. Put the paper in the machine, face down
  b. After that, dial the number
  c. When you hear the tone, push "send."
  Process: Sending a fax

Unit 13 – *Get ready!* (Student C)

Pantomime these actions. Your partners will guess what you are doing.

65

You are... 1. ...typing a letter.
  2. ...buying a newspaper.
  3. ...walking on a hot day.
  4. ...coming into the room.
  5. ...shaking hands with the president.

Unit 12 - Group Work (Travel Agent 3)

66

Does the hotel have	a swimming pool? restaurants? air-conditioning?	Yes, it does. No, it doesn't.
Where is the hotel located?		It's on the beach.
How far is it from the town center?		It's only a 15 minute walk.
Are meals tours included (in the package)?		Yes, breakfast is included. No, they aren't included.
How much does the tour cost?		Two thousand dollars including air-fare.

1 You are a travel agent. You work for World Travel Service. Tell customers about your company's tour to Mystic Island. You want them to buy your tour.

Hotel Traveler ★ (budget hotel)

★ Clean rooms, fans
★ Coffee shop
★ Morning coffee included
★ Free tour of Bazaar (famous market)

★ Location: in the heart of the famous Bazaar shopping and restaurant area in the town center; 10-minute walk to White Sands Beach; 5-minute walk to the nightlife area.
★ Price: $ 2,100 (including air-fare)

WORLD TRAVEL

Keep going!

2 Change parts. Travel agents become customers. Customers become agents. Ask the agents about tours to a place in your country. Decide which tour you want to take.

Review, Units 10-18 (Student A)

67 Talking tasks.
Read each card. Do the task with B.

1
- Think of a well-known place. Don't tell B the place. Give directions from here to the place. B will guess.
- Now listen to B's directions. Guess the place.

2
- You work for Horizon Travel. B will call you. Your manager, Ms. Johnson, isn't at her desk now. Find out B's phone number and take a message.
- B works for Union Bank. You need to send a letter. Call B. Find out the bank's

3
You and B are going to another country. What should you do before you go? Think of at least five things.
   We should...
   We have to...
   We need to...

4
- You work at the front desk of the Grand Hotel. B is a guest. B will call you. Respond.
- You took a tour. A lot of things went wrong. Think of at least four. B is your travel agent. Say your complaints.

5
How many things are you and B doing right now?
   We're sitting in class.
   We're speaking English.
Think of at least eight more things.

6
- Find three things you and B are both going to do during the next vacation.
- Then find three things B is going to do that you aren't.

How many spaces?

68 Use this box to decide how many spaces for the game.
1. Close your eyes.
2. Touch the "How many spaces" box with a pencil.
3. Move that many spaces.

How many spaces?

1	3	2	1	2	1	3	1	1	2	1	3	1	2	1	2	1	2	3	1	2
2	1	3	1	3	1	2	1	3	1	2	1	2	1	2	3	1	2	2	3	2
2	3	2	1	4	1	1	2	5	3	1	2	1	2	1	2	3	4	2	3	1
3	1	1	2	1	3	1	2	1	2	1	2	3	1	2	1	3	2	1	2	1
1	3	2	1	2	1	3	1	1	2	1	3	1	2	1	2	1	2	3	1	2
2	1	3	1	3	1	4	1	3	1	2	1	5	1	2	3	1	2	2	3	2
2	3	2	1	3	1	1	2	1	3	1	2	1	2	1	2	3	1	4	3	1
3	1	1	2	1	3	1	2	1	2	1	2	3	1	2	1	3	2	1	2	1

Pair Work B 👥
May I speak to...

1 You and A will have eight telephone conversations.
Sit back-to-back so you can't see each other. Read each card.
Cards 1, 3, 5, 7 = A calls B. Cards 2, 4, 6, 8 = B calls A.
When you need addresses and telephone numbers, use your own.

1.

> You are a secretary.
> Your boss, Ms. Lee, is in a meeting right now.
> Begin by saying:
>   Good _____, Union Bank.
>   (morning)
> Ask if A wants
> ■ to call Ms. Lee again later?
> OR
> ■ Ms. Lee to call him/her back? Be sure to find out A's phone number:
>   _____-_____

2.

> A works for a company called United Technology.
> You need to send a letter to A.
> Find out the address.
> When A answers, say:
>   This is _____ from _____.
>   (name)   (company).
>   Could you tell me United Technology's address?

3.

> You are a travel agent. Begin by saying:
>   Sunshine Travel. May I help you?
> Answer A's questions.
>
> Time   Flight   Airline
>
> **To Mexico City (MEX)**
> 1010   AM 452   Aeromexico
> 1150   US 731   United Airlines
>
> **To Rio de Janeiro (RIO)**
> 0800   RG 833   Varig
> 1035   RG 837   Varig
>
> **To Taipei (TPE)**
> 0840   CX 2455   Cathy Pacific
> 1335   CI 17   China Air

4.

> A is a secretary at Century Trading. You want to talk to A's boss, Mr.Sato. When A answers, say:
>   This is _____ from _____.
>   (name)   (company).
>   Is Mr. Sato in?

5.

> You work for a company called InterTech. Begin by saying:
>   InterTech. May I help you?
> Answer A's question.

6.

> A works for Universal, Inc..
> You want to set the time for a meeting tomorrow. Find a time when you both are free. When A answers, say:
>   Hello. This is _____ from
>   (name)
>   _____. I was wondering if we
>   (company)
>   could set up a time to meet tomorrow.

7.

> You work for Eastern Printing Co. Begin by saying:
>   Good _____. Eastern.
>   (afternoon)
> Listen to A. Answer.
> Use your own schedule.

8.

> A is a travel agent.
> You want to go to Seoul, Korea.
> When A answers, say:
>   I'm calling about flights to Seoul.
>   What time do they leave?
> Find out what time flights are.
> Decide which one you want.

┌ ─ ─ *Keep going!* ─ ─ ➤

2 Think of three more messages. Call A.
Leave the messages. Write A's message.

Unit 16 – Group Work

70 Cut out this box. Fold it as the arrows show.

Problem:

Advice #1: I think you should …

Advice #2: Why don't you …

Advice #3: Have you tried …

Advice #4: How about …

Advice #5: If I were you, I'd …

Letter of application

When you apply for a job, you may have to write a letter of application.
This is an example:

February 23, (year)

Personnel Director
Century Trading
1490 Michigan Ave.
Chicago, IL 62941

Dear sir or madam:

I am applying for the position of office clerk which was advertised in the Honolulu Times of February 20.

I am enclosing my résumé. As you can see, I will graduate from Honolulu City College next June. My major is Business Administration. I can type, use a computer and speak Spanish and some Japanese.

I would appreciate the opportunity for an interview.

I look forward to hearing from you.

Sincerely,

Jerry Sanchez

enc.

Folding a business letter

72

■ Fold the bottom 1/3 of the letter up.
■ Next, fold the top 1/3 down.

Intertech
SOFTWARE
249 Ocean Street
Seattle
Washington 98239
U.S.A.

Phone: (206) 555-2378
Fax: (206) 555-3894

April 25, (year)

■ When you fold it this way, the first thing the reader sees is your company's name and letterhead.

Addressing an envelope

This is the envelope for the letter Roy Green wrote to Maki Ito (page 9). Notice the parts:

Return (writer's) address:
Writer's name
Company
Street address
City, postal code*, country

Address of the person getting the letter:
Title (Ms., Mr., etc.) and full name
Job title
Company
Street address
City, postal code*, country.

Roy Green
Intertech SOFTWARE
249 Ocean Street
Seattle Washington 98239 U.S.A.

Ms. Maki Ito

Manager

World Travel

1-7-32 Honcho, Chuo-ku

Osaka 541 Japan

* In the U.S.A., a postal code is called a "ZIP code."

Write the country's name only if you are sending a letter to a different country than the one you are in.

Unit 18 - Group Work
Cut these squares out of your book.

By _____, I'll... (year)	In _____ years, I'm going to... (number)
By the time I'm _____ years old, (number) I'm going to...	Someday, I'll...

Unit 15 Group Work
Cut these squares out of your book.
Do NOT mix the complaints and responses.

Complaint:	**Complaint:**	**Complaint:**
Excuse me. _____ _____	Pardon me. _____ _____	I'm sorry but there's a problem. _____ _____
Response:	**Response:**	**Response:**
I'm very sorry. I'll... _____ _____	I apologize. I'll... _____ _____	I'm sorry _____ (sir/ma'am) I'll.._____ _____